sweet seams
fun-loving patterns

Sew Pretty
T-Shirt
Dresses

More Than 25 Easy, Pattern-Free Designs for Little Girls

sixth&spring books NEW YORK

Dedication

To all the little girls in our lives who inspired us to create dresses that are as delightful and stylish as they are.

sixth&spring books

161 Avenue of the Americas, New York, NY 10013

Editorial Director JOY AQUILINO	Proofreader DARYL BROWER
Developmental Editor LISA SILVERMAN	Principal Illustrator JOHN BAUMGARTEL
Art Director DIANE LAMPHRON	Photography DAN HOWELL
Design/Art Production Assistant LOIRA WALSH	Fashion Stylist EKATERINA SKNARINA
Instructions Writer and Samplemaker BETH BAUMGARTEL	Vice President, Publisher TRISHA MALCOLM
	Creative Director JOE VIOR
Consulting Editor MARTHA MORAN	Production Manager DAVID JOINNIDES
Copy Editor MICHELE FILON	President ART JOINNIDES

ISBN: 978-1-936096-49-7

Library of Congress Catalogue-in-Publication Data
is available from the Library of Congress

Manufactured in China

1 3 5 7 9 10 8 6 4 2

First Edition

✳ ✳ ✳ ✳ Contents

Here at Sweet Seams, we're pretty laid-back about most things, but we take our commitment to "fun-loving patterns" very seriously.

When we started our pattern line, we knew that we wanted to include designs for little girls' dresses. Not only are girls' dresses a lot of fun to sew, but we were inspired by the wonderful girls in our lives—daughters, nieces, granddaughters, god daughters—who all have a great sense of style and love to wear dresses we make especially for them.

We also knew that even avid stitchers don't always have time or money to spare. So we put our heads together and came up with a way to make sewing a special dress fun, easy, and affordable: Start with a T-shirt.

What could be easier? T-shirts are inexpensive, and chances are you'll find one that could work as a starting point for a dress in your little girl's closet. If you start with a T-shirt that she's worn before, you know right from the start how well it fits. You can use one that still fits in the shoulders and chest but is a little too short, or one that's stained near the hem, which you need to cut off in order to attach a skirt. Another benefit to upcycling a T-shirt into a dress is that there aren't any tricky necklines or sleeves to contend with, zippers to insert, or buttonholes to stitch. Plus, none of the designs in this book requires a pattern. We've provided general sizing and yardage guidelines for girls aged 2 to 8, but all the fabric requirements, cutting measurements, and sewing instructions can be adapted to any size T-shirt you're working with.

Once we began to explore style, shape, technique, color, and print, we quickly realized that the creative possibilities are virtually endless. The twenty-eight playful, stylish designs in this book feature gathers, ruffles, pleats, sashes, overskirts, aprons, flowers, bows, appliqués, and more, and range from sporty to trendy, from sweet to sassy, and from retro to positively regal. All use materials that are easy to find, and stitchers at every level of skill and experience can find designs they can easily achieve.

We hope this book inspires you transform an ordinary T-shirt into an extraordinary dress, that you enjoy sewing it, and—most important—that a special little girl in your life enjoys wearing it.

T-Shirt Dresses 101

Choosing the T-shirt and Fabric

The good news is that you probably already have everything you need to make these projects. You can repurpose an old T-shirt and many of the projects require less than a yard of fabric. Check the bottom of the T-shirt drawer and your fabric stash before heading to the store.

Selecting a T-shirt

A well-made cotton or cotton/polyester blend T-shirt that maintains its shape is the best choice. If the shirt has stretched or shrunk, it's not going to look any better as a dress than it did as T-shirt. All except very lightweight T-shirts, which won't support the weight of the skirt) will work for these projects.

Thinking about Size

For the shirt: Try the T-shirt on the child. If desired, choose a slightly larger shirt than usual to make the dress extra-comfortable. (Some of the patterns call for a slightly larger T-shirt for a loose-fitting dress.)

For the skirt: The following chart provides standard body measurements for different sizes. Adjust the cutting length of the skirt for your child by measuring the length of a favorite skirt and using that measurement to cut the skirt fabric (remember to add 1" to 2" for seam and hem allowances). Each project indicates cutting lengths for the T-shirt and the skirt fabric.

Measurement Chart

Size	S (2/3)	M (4/5)	L (6/6x)	XL (7/8)
Chest	22"	23"	25"	27"
Waist	20"	21"	22"	23"
Back waist length	8½"	9½"	10½"	12½"
Height	38"	41"	47"	52"

Choosing the Fabric

Most of the skirts in this book are made with woven fabrics, but knit fabrics can also be used (page 9). Woven fabrics don't stretch and are generally very easy to work with, especially quilting cottons, which can be found in a variety of fabulous prints. Woven fabrics come in different weights, so select a light- to medium-weight cotton or silk, or a lightweight linen. If you add an overskirt, be sure to keep the underskirt fabric lighter weight than the overskirt. Bring the T-shirt with you when you shop for skirt fabric to match colors and test the skirt fabric weight against it.

Cutting the T-shirt and Fabric

Before cutting, wash, dry and press the shirt and fabric in the same way you will launder the finished garment.

Cutting the T-shirt

Each project tells you where to cut the T-shirt to duplicate the look that is shown; adjust these measurements for the actual height of the child.

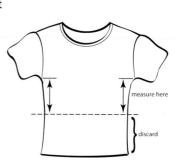

1. Lightly press the T-shirt.

2. Starting at the underarm seam on each side of the shirt, measure down the indicated cutting length and mark at the side seams with a fabric marker or chalk.

3. Use a ruler to draw a cutting line across the T-shirt connecting the two markings.

4. Cut along the marked line through both layers.

Cutting the Skirt Fabric

To duplicate the look of the dress as shown, follow the project cutting instructions.

• The length will be indicated; adjust this measurement to fit a shorter or taller child.

• To determine the cutting width, measure the circumference at the bottom edge of the cut T-shirt and multiply that measurement by 2", 2½", or 3" (2" for a moderately full skirt/ruffle and 3" for a very full skirt). In many cases, the result will be about 45", which is the width of many fabrics. If the result is greater than 45", you'll need to cut two fabric pieces and seam them, right sides together, using a ½" seam allowance.

For example: If the bottom circumference of the cut-off T-shirt is 20", one width of 45"-wide fabric will make a moderately gathered skirt. For a fuller skirt, seam together one full fabric width + an additional 17" (cut to the same length). This includes extra seam allowance to stitch the two widths together.

1. Press the fabric.

2. Trim the top edge as straight as possible. Cut the fabric so the length of the skirt is along the straight grain (parallel to the finished selvage edges) to ensure that the skirt hangs straight.

3. Measure and mark the desired length from the top edge at several intervals across the fabric width using fabric chalk, a fabric marking pen or straight pins. Use a long ruler to connect the markings.

4. Cut along the marked line.

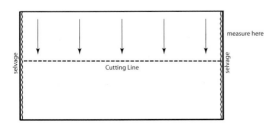

5. Repeat if you need a second width of fabric to obtain the desired skirt/ruffle fullness. Seam the two widths together along the straight grain.

Tools and Supplies

You won't need a lot of specialized tools to make these dresses, but the right ones will make sewing much easier and give you professional-looking results.

Basic Tool Kit
• matching thread
• dressmaker's chalk or fabric marking pen
• fabric scissors
• seam ripper
• ruler and measuring tape
• sewing machine, bobbins and extra needles
• straight pins
• hand sewing needles
• iron and ironing board

Sewing Machine

As long as your sewing machine sews straight and zigzag stitches, you can make any dress in this book. Seams that need to stretch will benefit from a stretch stitch (or small zigzag), but for the most part a basic straight stitch is all you need.

NEEDLES

Start each project with a new needle. Keep a selection of sizes on hand for different weights and types of fabric (fine needles for lightweight fabrics like chiffon and tulle, thicker needles for heavyweight fabrics); the smaller the number size, the finer the needle. Many of the projects feature quilting cottons and needle sizes 11/70 or 12/80 are suitable. A universal or sharp-point needle is suitable for most fabrics, especially wovens. If you're adding a knit fabric bottom to the T-shirt (see project on page 100), use a ballpoint needle so the rounded tip will slip more easily through it.

If at any time your stitch appears irregular, change the needle and rethread the machine. It's surprising how these simple steps fix many stitch problems.

PRESSER FEET AND ATTACHMENTS

Almost every machine comes with an assortment of presser feet and you can usually purchase additional specialty feet. The **general-purpose foot** is ideal for most sewing, but there are a few feet that are very helpful for specific tasks.

Use a **zipper foot** to cover cording when making piping and to apply piping in seams.

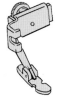

The shape of the **embroidery foot** allows it to move over dense stitching, such as satin stitches used to secure appliqués (see project on page 73).

Most of the projects require gathering lengths of fabric. A **gathering foot** is ideal for gathering a single layer or attaching and gathering two layers at the same time.

A **ruffler** is an attachment that makes uniform gathers or tiny pleats and does the same job as a gathering foot.

Other Sewing Tools

Insert **straight pins** every few inches, or even closer; the more you use, the less the fabrics will shift as you sew. Insert your pins perpendicular to the edge of the fabric so they're easy to remove as you sew.

Keep several **hand-sewing needles** on hand for tacking on trim and finishing work.

You'll need 7" or 8" **dressmaker shears** for cutting T-shirts and fabric. **Smaller embroidery scissors** or thread snips are helpful for trimming seams and clipping threads. **Pinking shears** are a great way to trim and edge finish seams that might otherwise ravel.

Accurate measuring is important. A 2"-or 3"-wide **transparent ruler** is idea for measuring and marking straight cutting lines, while a **tape measure** can measure around curves.

You can mark cutting lines and length and width measurements directly on most fabrics with **dressmaker's chalk** or **fabric markers**, although you should test first on a scrap or corner. Chalk lines can be brushed off and lines made with water-soluble markers will disappear when water is applied.

Have a **seam ripper** on hand—just in case!

Notions

It's fun to have an assortment of **trims and novelties**. Each project specifies the notions needed to make the garment, but when you're out and about and spot great trims, it's a good idea to pick them up. You'll use them eventually and you never know what might make the perfect finishing touch.

Cotton/polyester blend **thread** is suitable for most sewing. 100% polyester also works because it stretches. Avoid 100% cotton for knit fabrics because it doesn't stretch. Always keep white and black thread on hand.

In addition to elastic in various widths, these novelty notions and trims are nice to have on hand:

• decorative buttons

• rickrack in a variety of widths

• single-fold and double-fold bias binding

• band trims such as ribbons, braid, and gimp

• edging trims such as eyelet, fringe, ruffling, piping, and ball fringe

Keep all your fabric scraps! You never know when an old scrap will make the perfect hem band, appliqué, or bias trim.

Basic Sewing Stitches

The following machine stitches are all you need to make the dresses in this book.

Backstitch for about an inch at the beginning and end of each seam to keep the thread ends from unraveling.

Basting, the longest machine stitch, has two purposes: it holds layers together temporarily or it gathers a length of fabric.

An **edgestitch** is a permanent stitch, visible on the right side, stitched as close as possible to a folded edge.

Staystitching is a row of straight stitches through a single layer of fabric, usually done along a curved edge (or along the straight edge of a knit fabric) within the seam allowance to prevent stretching.

If the T-shirt you are working with tends to stretch a lot, staystitch the bottom edge after you cut it.

A **topstitch** is a decorative stitch that is meant to be seen; embroidery or contrast color threads make it even more visible.

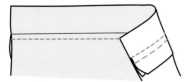

The **zigzag** stitch is particularly important when working with knitted fabrics because it stretches. Use a narrow zigzag when sewing the skirt to the bottom of the T-shirt. It is also used as an edge finish to prevent raveling, and to secure appliqués. Vary the length and width for different results; a shorter zigzag looks like a satin stitch and is perfect for stitching appliqués, while a wider stitch is better for decorative stitching.

Basic Sewing Techniques

There are certain basic sewing techniques that you will use over and over again as you sew the projects in this book. Unless otherwise indicated, all seams in this book are sewn with straight stitches set at 8 to 12 stitches per inch (2.5 cm), and ½" seam allowances.

Pressing

Pressing is the key to successful sewing. Press every seam you sew to ensure flat, smooth seams.

To press, smooth the seam with your hands, press the iron onto the seam and then lift the iron and move it to a new section and repeat. Press every seam flat right after you sew it. Unless otherwise specified, press both seam allowances to one side and generally to the back of the garment. Pressing is particularly important when sewing the skirt bottoms to the knit shirts. Don't move the iron back and forth (that's ironing, and should only be done on flat fabric and finished garments).

Working with Knit Fabrics

The great thing about knit fabrics is that they don't have to fit perfectly because they stretch. Since these T-shirt dresses all have knit tops you don't have to worry about zippers or buttonholes.

Here are some tips for sewing knits. It's best to use a stretch stitch. If your machine doesn't have a stretch stitch, don't worry, use a narrow zigzag stitch instead, and follow these tips:

• Knit fabric stretches and so should the stitching.

• If the cut edge of the T-shirt rolls, spray it with starch and press it gently.

• Install a new, ballpoint needle in your machine before beginning work.

• Stitch with a longer stitch length (9 per inch).

• Gently stretch the seam as you stitch.

• If you have a serger, use it to stitch and edge-finish knit fabrics at the same time.

Stitching Woven Skirts to Knit Tops

In most instances you'll be stitching a woven bottom to a knit top, using either a stretch or a zigzag stitch.

1. Staystitch (page 9) the bottom edge of the T-shirt within the seam allowance. Take care to avoid stretching the fabric.

2. Use many pins to hold the layers together and ensure that the knit layer doesn't distort during stitching.

3. Every few inches, stop and lift the presser foot as you stitch to avoid distortion and fabric creeping.

Working with Sheer Fabrics

Several dresses are made with overskirts sheer fabrics like chiffon, organza, and tulle. Here are a few tips that will make cutting and sewing these special fabrics easier.

• Pin or tape sheer fabrics to a cutting mat or a piece of foamcore to minimize slippage while cutting. Since the fabric will be gathered, small imperfections in cutting will be hidden in the layers.

• Start with a new, finer needle (try size 9/60 or 10/70) and set your machine for a short stitch length.

• Hold the thread ends as you begin sewing.

• Stop sewing every 6" and leave the needle down; lift the presser foot to release any tension in the fabric. Continue sewing, taking care not to push or pull the fabric.

A **French seam** is a seam and seam finish all in one and it's ideal for sheer fabrics. Allow ⅜" seam allowance.

1. Sew a ⅜" seam with the wrong sides together. Trim the seam allowance to ⅛".

2. Turn the seam inside out so the right sides are together and the narrow seam allowance is sandwiched between the fabric layers; press.

3. Sew the seam again using a ¼" seam allowance to encase the raw edges. Turn the garment right side out and press.

Refer to the narrow hem (page 11) for the best way to hem chiffon and organza, which can shift as you sew. Tulle should be left unhemmed.

Turning Corners

Slow down as you approach a corner. Stop with the needle down when you are ½" from the edge of the fabric. Lift the presser foot and pivot the fabric. Lower the presser foot and continue stitching.

For heavier weight fabric, round the corner by taking two diagonal stitches.

Trimming, Clipping, and Notching Seam Allowances

Before seam finishing, trim, clip, and notch as needed to reduce bulk and ease the seam allowance so it lays flat. Take special care not to cut through the stitching

when clipping or notching. On tight curves, clip or notch about every ½"; on gentler curves every 1".

Trim the seam allowances to about ¼" to reduce bulk.

Clip small snips into the seam allowances of inwardly curved seams and cut out small notches of outwardly curves seams.

Clean-Finishing Seam Allowances

It's a good idea to clean-finish the seam allowances so they don't ravel and create a rat's nest of threads on the inside when laundered.

Pinked Seam Finish: Trim away the excess seam allowance with pinking shears. The zigzag cut edge won't ravel and makes a soft, comfortable edge after washing. If the fabric ravels a lot, stitch ¼" from each raw edge before you pink the edges.

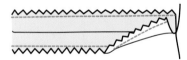

Zigzag Seam Finish: Press the seam open and stitch a narrow zigzag along the cut edge of each seam allowance. On lightweight fabrics, you can zigzag the seam allowances together.

Overlock Finish: If you have a serger, you already know it's the quickest and easiest way to finish seam allowances. And it trims the seam allowance as it overlocks the cut edge.

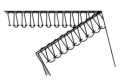

Narrow-Hemming

Since most of these projects are casual dresses, machine hemming is the way to go. And in most instances, unless otherwise indicated, a narrow hem is the easiest and most suitable. Here are three ways to do it; Method 3 is particularly suited to sheers.

Method 1: Trim the hem allowance to ½" and zigzag or overlock the cut edge. Press the hem allowance to the wrong side and machine edgestitch it in place.

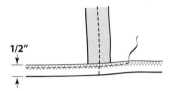

Method 2: Trim the hem allowance to ½". Press ¼" to the wrong side and then ¼" again. Machine edgestitch close to the inner fold.

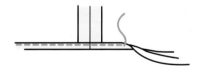

Method 3: Mark the hemline and trim the hem allowance to ½". Press the hem allowance to the wrong side on the marked hemline. With the right side up, narrow zigzag along the fabric fold. Carefully trim away the excess hem allowance.

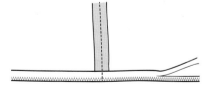

Gathering

Gathering is a way of sewing a larger width of fabric to a smaller width with a series of soft folds. It's also used to make ruffles. There are several ways to gather fabric. Consider trying all the methods to find the easiest and quickest way for you.

When joining two or more strips together to obtain the desired width (see page 7), mark both sections to ensure evenly distributed gathers.

Many projects require gathering, and gathering uses a lot of thread, so make extra bobbins with white thread. You don't want to have to stop mid-project to wind a new bobbin.

MARKING FOR GATHERING
For most of the projects in this book, you will be gathering the top edge of the skirts to the bottom edges of the T-shirts. The key to even gathering is careful marking.

1. Fold the T-shirt in half lengthwise to find the center front and center back.

2. If the skirt has one seam, make it the center back; if there are two seams make them the side seams. Fold the skirt in half and in half again, positioning the seams as desired.

3. Make a chalk mark or insert a straight pin at all the folds on the T-shirt and on the skirt to mark the center front, center back and sides (or halfway between the centers).

SEWING MACHINE GATHERING WITH BASTING STITCHES
1. Working on the right side of the fabric, baste two rows of straight, long, parallel stitches in the seam allowance; one just inside the stitching line and the other ¼" away. Be sure to leave long thread tails. Secure one end of the thread tails so they don't pull out accidentally.

2. Pull the loose bobbin thread tails to gather the fabric, sliding the fabric along the threads. Loosen the tension on the needle thread so the bobbin threads are easier to pull.

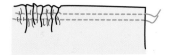

3. When the gathered piece matches the length of the corresponding ungathered piece, pin the layers together, adjusting the gathers so they are evenly distributed. Change to a shorter stitch length and stitch the two layers together.

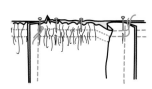

If the fabric to be gathered is long, divide it in halves or quarters and baste and gather each section independently.

SEWING MACHINE GATHERING WITH ZIGZAG STITCHES
This technique works well with heavier fabrics.

1. Position a length of yarn or narrow cording just inside the seam allowance and set your machine for a wide zigzag stitch.

2. Center the presser foot over the yarn or cording and zigzag directly over it making sure the stitches don't go through the yarn/cording.

3. Gently pull the yarn/cording to gather the fabric. Make sure you don't accidentally pull it through the stitches.

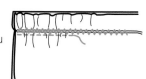

4. When the gathered piece matches the corresponding piece, pin the layers together, adjusting the gathers so they are evenly distributed. Change to a shorter stitch length and stitch the two layers together.

SEWING MACHINE GATHERING WITH A GATHERING FOOT OR A RUFFLER
A gathering presser foot or ruffler attachment (page 8) speeds up the gathering process. They are both available for most sewing machine brands. Refer to the manufacturer's instructions, but be sure to test on scrap fabric first and to play around with machine settings and possible adjustments.

GATHERING WITH A SERGER

Differential feed is the serger setting that makes it possible for the machine to gather fabric as it finishes the cut edge. Since every serger is a bit different and you are using a variety of fabric weights, practice on scrap fabric first. Refer to your instruction manual as well.

1. Set the differential feed to the highest setting.

2. Set the stitch length to the highest setting for the longest stitch.

3. Set needles at the highest tension setting. (The lower the thread tensions, the fewer the gathers.)

4. Keep the looper settings at an average setting, or one number higher than average (around 4 to 5).

5. Loosen the pressure foot adjuster (usually above the presser foot). Or, if you have a gathering foot, replace the standard foot.

6. Once you're satisfied with the settings, insert the fabric under the presser foot and let the serger pull the edge through the machine, gathering it as it overlocks the edge.

7. If you do have a gathering foot, you can gather and attach layers at the same time. The layer to be gathered goes under the presser foot and the non-gathered layer goes through the top section of the foot. Refer to the manufacturer's instructions.

Gathering with a serger requires trial and error. Make note of the serger settings directly on a fabric scrap once you're satisfied with the stitch and keep it for reference.

Making Ruffles

Straight ruffles are softly gathered rectangular strips of fabric. Variety is created in the way they are attached to the garment.

BASIC STRAIGHT RUFFLE

This can be a single layer that's narrow-hemmed on the lower edge (see below left) or a double layer ruffle (see below right). The upper edge of both a single or double layer ruffle is gathered as above and stitched to the garment.

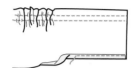 

DOUBLE RUFFLE

1. Cut a strip of fabric (the desired width + ½") x (the desired length x 2). Stitch multiple fabric strips with the right sides together to obtain the desired length.

2. Narrow-hem, overlock, or zigzag stitch all edges.

3. Run two rows of gathering stitches through the center of the strip. Pull the gathering stitches until the ruffle is the desired length and the gathers are evenly distributed.

4. Pin the ruffle, wrong side down, to the right side  of the garment and stitch between the rows of basting stitches. Remove the basting stitches.

RUFFLE WITH HEADING

1. First narrow-hem (page 11) the ruffle's long edges and run two rows of gathering stitches at the top edge of the ruffle.

2. Trim the seam allowance of the garment edge to which the ruffle will be applied to ¼". Pin the wrong sides of the ruffle and garment 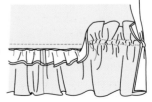 together with the bottom row of gathering stitches aligned with the garment seam line.

3. Adjust the gathers and stitch close to the bottom of the gathers.

4. Press the ruffle up and over the stitching, enclosing the raw edge. Stitch the ruffle to the right side of the garment, close to the top row of gathers. Remove the basting.

Applying Flat Trim

You can always hand-stitch trim in place, but it's so quick and easy to stitch it by machine.

1. Secure the trim in the desired location with lots of pins, basting tape, or even fabric adhesive.

2. If the trim is narrow, simply run one row of straight machine stitches down the center. This typically works with rickrack, soutache, and narrow ribbon.

3. If the trim is wider than ¼", machine stitch both long edges. To avoid puckers, stitch both edges in the same direction.

4. To apply flat trim or edging to the hem of a garment, position the wrong side of the garment over the edge of the trim and edgestitch close to the fold.

Making and Applying Bias Binding

You can buy premade bias binding, but it's easy to make your own when you have a decorative fabric.

1. Mark the bias grainline at a 45° angle to the selvage.

2. Mark and cut strips of fabric parallel to the bias grain. Mark them four times (for double fold) or two times (for single fold) as wide as the desired width.

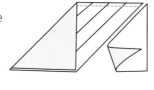

3. Piece the strips together as needed by stitching the narrow ends at right angles

with the right sides together. Stitch diagonally from corner to corner. Trim the seam allowances and press the seam flat.

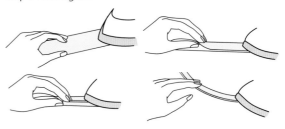

4. Press both long edges to the center of the strip for single-fold binding. For double-fold binding, press the strip in half again.

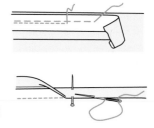

5. To apply single-fold bias binding, press one long edge of the bias binding open and pin it to the cut edge of the garment with the right sides together. Stitch directly over the pressed fold line. Wrap the binding to the wrong side and slipstitch or edgestitch it in place.

6. To apply double-fold bias binding, with the right side facing up, slide the cut edge of the garment between the two sides of the binding. Machine-stitch along the inside folded edge, making sure to simultaneously catch the underlayer.

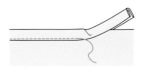

Making and Applying Piping

Making your own piping is easy, and you're sure to get the right color when you use your fabric scraps.

1. Cut bias strips of fabric as for bias binding that are equal in width to two times the seam allowance (1")

plus the circumference of the cord you plan to cover. Allow enough length to overlap the ends.

2. Attach the zipper foot. Wrap the bias strip, right side out, around the cording with cut edges even. Stitch close to the cord, stretching the fabric slightly as you stitch.

3. Attach the zipper foot. Baste the piping to the right side of one of the fabric sections along the seam line, with all cut edges aligned. Pin the other section over the piping right sides together and stitch on the seam line through all the thicknesses.

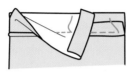

Making Fabric Sash Belts or Hair Ties

Depending on the weight of the fabric, you can make a single layer or a double layer sash or hair tie. Both are suitable for a little girl's dress. To determine the best length, tie a tape measure or fabric scrap around the child's waist (or around her hairline) and use that as a guide. The width will vary depending on the style of the dress, but most fabric sashes are between 1½" and 4" wide.

MAKING A DOUBLE FABRIC SASH BELT
Length: desired length + 1"
Width: double the desired width + 1"

1. Fold the fabric with the right sides together. Stitch the short edges and long edge, leaving a 3" opening for turning on the long edge.

2. Trim the seam allowances and turn the sash right side out. Press the seam allowances at the opening to the wrong side.

3. Edgestitch all around the sash, closing the opening in the stitching. If desired, stitch the narrow ends at an angle, as shown. Trim the ends.

MAKING A SINGLE FABRIC SASH BELT
1. Piece together narrow strips (usually between 2" to 4" wide) as needed to obtain the desired length.

2. Narrow-hem (page 11) all the sides of the strip and press. You might want to secure the sash to the dress at the center back or side seams.

Working with the Templates

While none of the dress designs in this book requires a pattern, a few feature elements such as pockets and appliqués that do. You'll find templates for these on the following pages.

To use a template, start by photocopying the page on which it appears at same size (100%) on standard-weight photocopy/printer paper. In most cases you'll need to make only one copy; for the pennants and flowers for the Banner Day project (see project on page 96), you'll want to make multiples so you can speed up the cutting process.

Cut out the photocopied template, position it on your fabric, and pin it in place before cutting the fabric.

For the scalloped edge template on page 17 (see the Tea Party project on page 67), you'll need to trace it onto a piece of cardboard before using it to cut the T-shirt.

Pocket template for
Bright and Bouncy, page 20

✱ All templates
shown at 100%

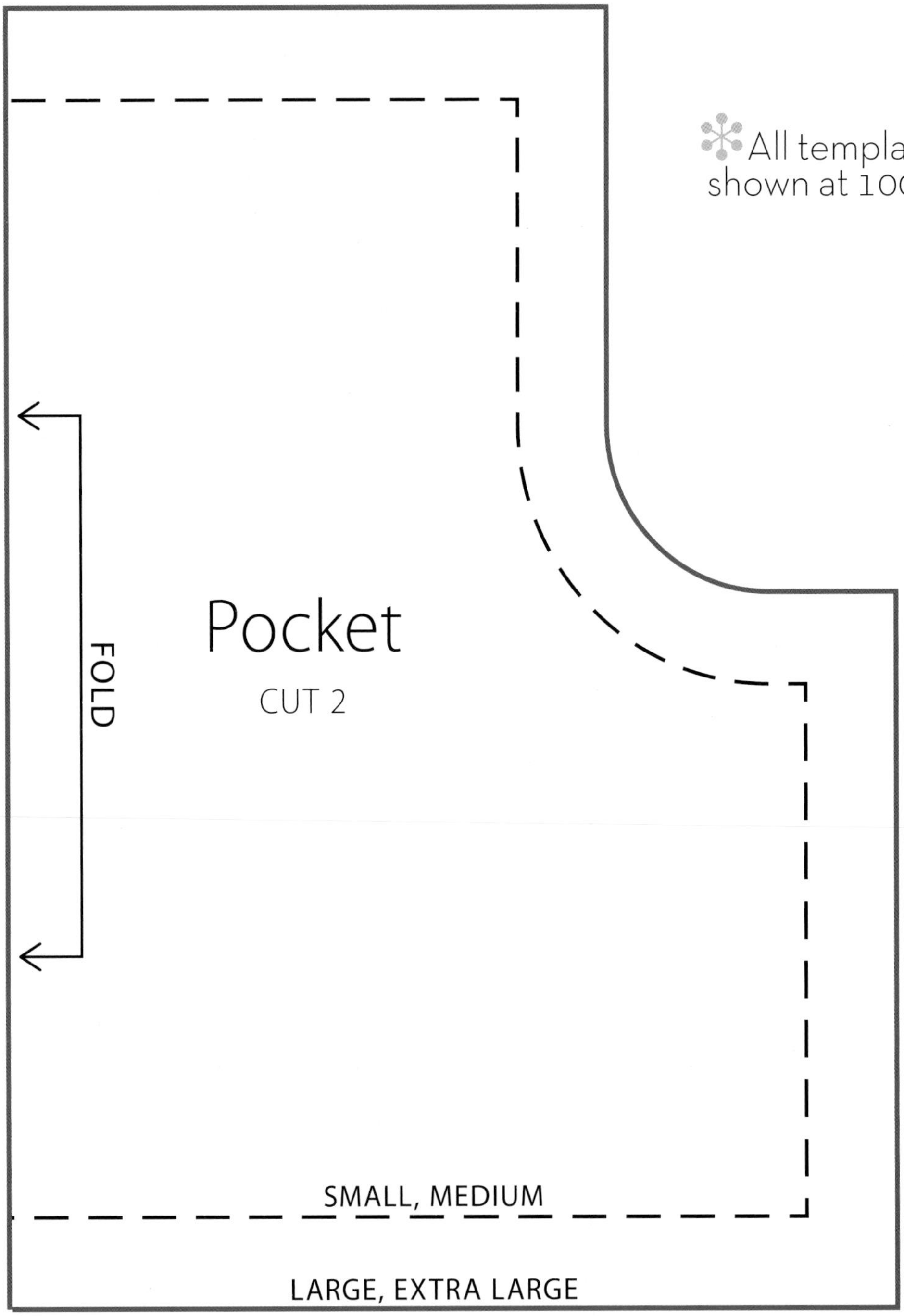

FOLD

Pocket

CUT 2

SMALL, MEDIUM

LARGE, EXTRA LARGE

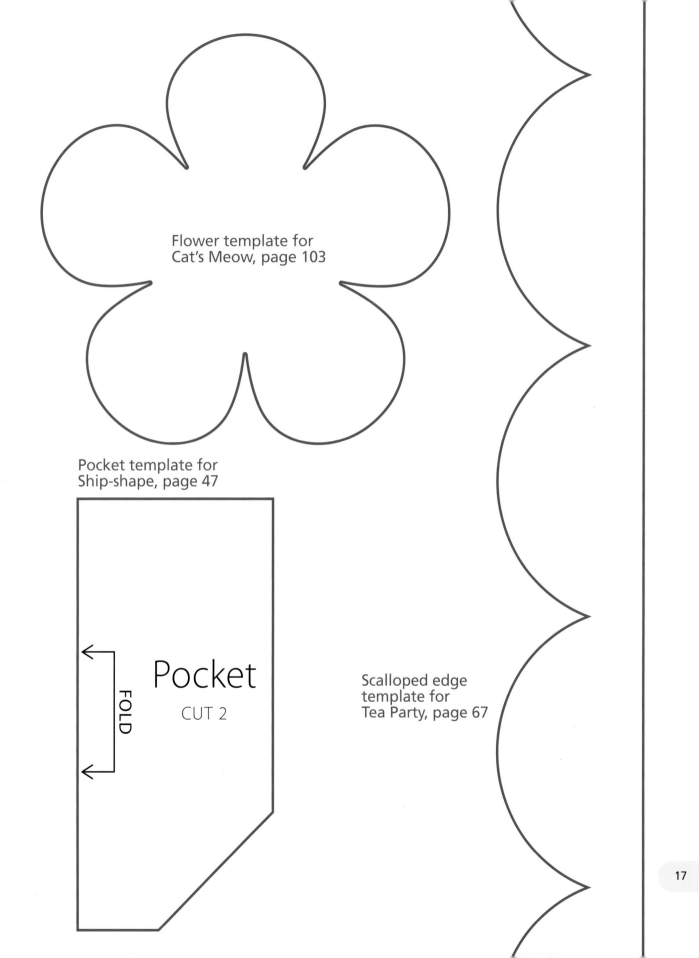

Flower template for
Cat's Meow, page 103

Pocket template for
Ship-shape, page 47

Pocket

FOLD

CUT 2

Scalloped edge
template for
Tea Party, page 67

✳ All templates shown at 100%

Peace sign template for
Feeling Groovy, page 73

Banner and flower
templates for
Banner Day, page 96

Flower
CUT 12

Banner CUT 60 (approx.)

18

PHOTOCOPYING OF TEMPLATE PERMITTED

Sew Pretty T-Shirt Projects

As you can see from this collection of darling dresses,
there are no limits when it comes to transforming a T-shirt into
something fun, wearable, and unique.

Let the color of the T-shirt, the fabric you find at your local fabric
or quilting store (or in your stash), and the little girl who inspires
you to sew be your guides. Happy sewing!

Bright and Bouncy

Two big ruffles at the hem make a T-shirt fun—and a kangaroo pocket makes it practical. To make this dress the right length, start with a larger T-shirt.

Spots and stripes are perfect for playdates

What You'll Need:

● Basic tool kit (page 7)

● Long T-shirt (one size larger than the child usually wears)

● For the ruffles and pocket: see yardage chart (right)

● Pocket template (page 16)

Instructions are for sizes Small (Medium, Large, Extra-Large). Sample shown in size Small.

All seam allowances are ½" unless otherwise noted.

45"-wide fabric	S (2/3) / M (4/5)	L (6/6x) / XL (7/8)
	½ yard	¾ yard

Getting Ready

1 Cut away the hemmed edge of the T-shirt.

2 For sizes Small and Medium, the cutting width of the ruffles is a full crossgrain of fabric (about 45"). For sizes Large and Extra-Large, determine the cutting width of the ruffles by measuring the circumference at the bottom edge of the T-shirt and multiplying by 2 (you'll need to cut two pieces, stitch them together at one short end, and trim to the desired size). Cut the fabric for the ruffles as follows:

	S (2/3)/M(4/5)	L (6/6x)/XL(7/8)
Top ruffle	Cutting width x 3" long	Cutting width x 4" long
Bottom ruffle	Cutting width x 4" long	Cutting width x 5" long

For the pocket, cut two pieces of fabric using the template provided (see page 16).

Bright and Bouncy

Sewing the Dress

3 With right sides together, sew the pocket pieces together around all edges, leaving a 4" opening along the bottom edge. Trim the seam allowance and corners and turn the pocket right side out. Press the entire pocket, turning the open seam allowances to the inside (the opening will be stitched shut when pocket is stitched to the T-shirt).

4 Try the T-shirt on the child to determine the pocket placement. Position and pin the pocket to the center of the T-shirt at the desired position. Edgestitch the pocket in place along the top edge, the straight side edges, and the bottom edge, backstitching at each end of each stitching line. Do not stitch the curved edges.

5 With right sides together, make the top and bottom ruffles by stitching the short ends together to form circles. Narrow-hem (see page 11) the bottom edge of each ruffle.

6 Pin the wrong side of the shorter (top) ruffle to the right side of the longer (bottom) ruffle so the top edges and seams are aligned. Run two rows of gathering stitches along the top edges through both layers (see pages 11–12 for how to gather). Measure and mark the center front, center back, and sides of both the lower edge of the T-shirt and the top edge of the ruffles (see page 12).

7 Gather the ruffles and pin them to the bottom of the T-shirt with right sides together and the markings aligned. Adjust the gathers and stitch. Press the seam toward the T-shirt. Remove any visible gathering stitches.❄

❋ ❋ ❋ ❋

Sunny Day

It's a good thing this dress can be sewn up in little more than an hour—she'll definitely want more than one in her closet.

What You'll Need:
- Basic tool kit (page 7)
- T-shirt
- For the top tier: ¼ yard 45"-inch wide fabric
- For the middle tier: ½ yard 45"-inch wide fabric
- For the bottom tier: ½ yard 45"-inch wide fabric
- 1¾ (1¾, 2¾, 2¾) yards pompom trim
- Zipper foot

Instructions are for sizes Small (Medium, Large, Extra-Large). Sample shown in size Small. All seam allowances are ½" unless otherwise noted.

Soak up the sunshine in an easy-peasy dress

Getting Ready

1 Lay the T-shirt out flat, measure and mark 3" (3", 3½", 4") down from each underarm seam, and follow the cutting instructions on page 6. Mark the center front and center back of the shirt.

2 Cut the skirt fabric as follows:

	S (2/3)	M (4/5)	L (6/6x)	XL (7/8)
Top tier	(1) 4½" x 36"	(1) 5" x 36"	(1) 5½" x 41"	(1) 6" x 45"
Middle tier	(1) 5½" x 45"	(1) 6" x 45"	(2) 6½" x 30"	(2) 7" x 34"
Bottom tier	(2) 6½" x 30"	(2) 7" x 30"	(2) 7½" x 40"	(2) 8" x 44"

Sewing the Dress

3 With right sides together, sew the two pieces for the bottom tier together along the short edges to make a circle. Run two rows of gathering stitches along the top edge (see pages 11–12 for how to gather). Measure and mark the top edge (page 12) for gathering. Overlock or zigzag along the bottom edge; press the stitched edge ½" to the wrong side and edgestitch it in place. Pin the header of the pompom trim to the wrong side of the hemmed edge so it isn't visible from the right side and the pompoms extend below the hem. Attach the zipper foot and stitch the trim in place close to the lower edge.

Sunny Day

4 For sizes Large and Extra-Large, sew the two pieces for the middle tier together along the short edges to form a circle. For sizes Small and Medium, sew the short edges together so that the middle tier forms a circle. Run two rows of gathering stitches along the top edge. Measure and mark the center front and side seams on the top and bottom edge. Run two rows of gathering stitches along the top edge.

5 With right sides together, pin the top edge of the bottom tier to the bottom edge of the middle tier, adjusting the gathers so they're evenly distributed. Stitch.

6 With right sides together, stitch the top tier to form a circle. Run gathering stitches along the top edge and measure and mark as for the other tiers. As in step 5, pin, adjust the gathers, and stitch the top edge of the middle tier to the bottom edge of the top tier.

7 As in previous steps, pull the gathering stitches of the top tier to fit the bottom of the T-shirt. Adjust the gathers, pin the skirt and top with right sides together, and stitch. ✳

✳ ✳ ✳ ✳

Past Perfect

Here's a lovely and unique way to create a vintage look lace doilies. Embellish each doily's center with a mother-of-pearl button, finish the skirt hem with a band of lace, and complete the look with delicate pearl "necklaces."

A vintage beauty in pearls and lace

What You'll Need:

- Basic tool kit (page 7)
- T-shirt
- For the skirt: ½ (½, ¾, ¾) yard 45"-wide fabric
- 10 to15 lace doilies (ours are 5" in diameter)
- 10 to 15 buttons (ours are ¾" in diameter)
- 2 yards 1½"-wide lace trim
- 1 yard each of three types of narrow-width pearl trim
- For the flower (optional)

Instructions are for sizes Small (Medium, Large, Extra-Large). Sample shown in size Small.

All seam allowances are ½" unless otherwise noted.

Getting Ready

1 Lay the T-shirt out flat, measure and mark 8" (8", 10", 10") down from each underarm seam, and follow the cutting instructions on page 6. Mark the center front and center back of the shirt.

2 Measure the circumference at the bottom edge of the shirt and multiply by 2. For all sizes simply use one fabric width. If the T-shirt bottom measures more than 22" and you want a fuller skirt, use ¾ yard of fabric. Refer to the chart below for the appropriate lengths for each size.

	S (2/3)	M (4/5)	L (6/6x)	XL (7/8)
Skirt length	9½"	10"	12½"	13"

Sewing the Dress

3 With right sides facing, sew the short edges of the skirt together (center back seam), then narrow-hem (page 11) the bottom edge. Measure and mark the center front and side seams of the skirt (page 12). Run two rows of gathering stitches along the top edge (see pages 11–12 for how to gather).

4 Position the doilies randomly around the skirt and pin them in place, arranging some to extend over the top edge of the skirt. Loosely machine- or handstitch the edges of the doilies to secure them to the skirt.

Past Perfect

5 If the lace trim is flat, gather the straight edge slightly with a row of gathering stitches. Edgestitch the top edge of the trim to the hem edge of the skirt, adjusting the gathers as you stitch to keep them even. Overlap the cut ends of the trim.

6 Pull the gathers along the top edge of the skirt so it fits the bottom of the T-shirt. Pin the T-shirt and skirt with right sides together, adjusting the gathers so the markings align and the gathers are evenly distributed. Stitch.

7 Handstitch a button to the center of each doily.

8 Arrange one of the pearl trims on the front of the T-shirt to resemble a necklace. Handstitch over the pearls between every three or four beads, starting and stopping at shoulder seams. Repeat with the two other trims to create "necklaces" of varying lengths.

9 To make the lace flower (optional), cut a piece of lace trim about 8" long. Run a gathering stitch along the lace's straight, long edge, then pull the gathers as tight as possible so the lace scrunches up to form a circle. Sew the short ends together. Sew a short length of pearl trim to fill in the center of the flower. Sew a pin back to the back.❈

Patchwork of Art

Use this project to introduce your little girl to the joys of beautiful fabric by letting her choose the colors and prints for the patchwork and the appliqué.

An oversized appliqué gives this design Boho beauty

What You'll Need:

- Basic tool kit (page 7)
- T-shirt
- For the skirt: 4 to 6 fat quarters
- For the hem band/lining: 1½ yards 45"-wide fabric
- To trim the skirt: 1½ yards eyelet trim
- Double-sided, paper-backed fusible web

Instructions are for sizes Small (Medium, Large, Extra-Large). Sample shown in size Medium. All seam allowances are ½" unless otherwise noted.

Note The finished measurements of each patchwork square in the instructions and the sample dress are 5" wide by 5½" long, and the finished depth of the hem band is 2". If you adjust these measurements to change the size and/or length of the dress, remember to adjust the dimensions of the hem band/lining accordingly.

Getting Ready

1 Hold the T-shirt up to your child to decide how much you want to cut off, or measure 8" down from each underarm seam. Follow the cutting instructions on page 6. Mark the center front and center back of the shirt.

2 Choose one fabric that has a suitable appliqué motif. Rough-cut around the motif, allowing at least 2" all around its perimeter. Set aside.

3 From the fat quarters, cut a total of twenty fabric squares, each 6" x 6½" (includes ½" seam allowance).

4 Cut the hem band and skirt lining as one 16" x 51" piece. (Adjust these dimensions as needed if you're working with different patchwork square or hem band measurements.) This will require stitching together two fabrics to obtain the desired width (unless your fabric is 54" wide).

Sewing the Dress

5 Lay out the patchwork squares in two rows of ten squares. With right sides together, sew ten squares into one strip, and the remaining ten into a second strip (see Figure A). Press the seam allowances open. With right sides together sew the two strips together for a finished piece that's ten squares wide by two squares long. Press the seam allowances open.

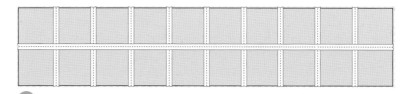

A

Patchwork of Art

6 Press one long edge of the hem band/lining 2½" to the wrong side. With right sides together, pin the long edge of the hem band/lining that is closest to the pressed crease to the bottom edge of the patchwork piece. Stitch, then fold the lining to the inside along the crease to create a 2"-hem band and a lined skirt.

7 Smooth the two layers together and baste the top edges together. Stitch the layers together to form the hem band by topstitching directly on top of the skirt/hem band seam (see Figure B).

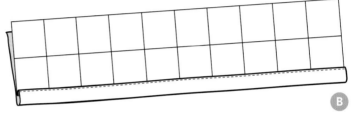

B

8 With right sides of the patchwork fabric together, pin the center back seam so it includes both the patchwork and lining fabrics. Stitch the center back seam and either zigzag or serge the seam allowances together and press them to one side.

9 Topstitch the top edge of the eyelet trim to the inside bottom edge of the skirt, starting at the center back seam and overlapping the cut ends of the eyelet.

10 Following the manufacturer's instructions, fuse the paper-backed fusible web to the rough-cut appliqué fabric. Cut out the motif exactly as you want it to appear on the T-shirt. Remove the backing paper and fuse the motif onto the T-shirt.

11 Sew two rows of basting stitches along the top edge of the skirt, through both layers (see pages 11–12 for how to gather). With right sides together, pin the top of the skirt to the bottom of the T-shirt, adjusting the gathers to fit (see Figure C). Set your sewing machine for a stretch or zigzag stitch and sew the seam. Serge or zigzag the seam allowances together and press them toward the shirt. ✣

Prep School

Give a plain polo shirt lots of little-girl style with a skirt made from several bands of classic print fabrics.

Get perfectly preppy with smart stripes

What You'll Need:
- Basic tool kit (page 7)
- Polo shirt
- For the skirt bands, sash, and/or hair tie: see the yardage chart (right)
- 2 packages jumbo rickrack

Instructions are for sizes Small (Medium, Large, Extra-Large). Sample shown in size Large. All seam allowances are ½" unless otherwise noted.

45"-wide fabric	S (2/3) / M (4/5)	L (6/6x) / XL (7/8)
Striped	½ yard	¾ yard
White	¼ yard	½ yard
Print	¼ yard	½ yard

Getting Ready

1 Lay the polo shirt out flat, measure and mark 4" (4½", 5", 5½") down from each underarm seam, and follow the cutting instructions on page 6. Mark the center front and center back of the shirt.

2 The dress shown features seven bands of fabric. For a longer dress, add one or more bands; to shorten, eliminate one or more bands. Cut the fabric as follows:

	S (2/3)	M (4/5)	L (6/6x)	XL (7/8)
Top band (striped)	(2) 8" x 26"	(2) 8½" x 26"	(2) 9" x 30"	(2) 9½" x 34"
Second band (white)	(2) 2" x 26"	(2) 2" x 26"	(2) 2½" x 30"	(2) 3" x 34"
Third band (print)	(2) 2" x 26"	(2) 2" x 26"	(2) 2½" x 30"	(2) 3" x 34"
Fourth band (white)	(2) 2" x 26"	(2) 2" x 26"	(2) 2½" x 30"	(2) 3" x 34"
Fifth band (print)	(2) 2½" x 26"	(2) 2½" x 26"	(2) 3" x 30"	(2) 3½" x 34"
Sixth band (white)	(2) 2" x 26"	(2) 2" x 26"	(2) 2½" x 30"	(2) 3" x 34"
Seventh band (print)	(2) 2½" x 26"	(2) 2½" x 26"	(2) 3" x 30"	(2) 3½" x 34"

Prep School

	S (2/3)/M (4/5)	L (6/6x)/XL (7/8)
Sash belt and/or hair tie (optional)	5½" x 45"	5½" x 55"

Sewing the Dress

3 Make all the bands by sewing the two pieces for each band with the right sides together along the shorter edges to make a circle. Then with the bands right sides together, sew the first five bands together. Refer to Step 2 and the photographs of the sample dress for the sequence.

4 Press the bottom edge of the fifth band ¼" to the wrong side and baste rickrack along the fold.

5 Stitch the sixth and seventh bands together with the right sides facing. Position the right side of the sixth band under the rickrack. Topstitch the fifth band, rickrack, and sixth band together along the basting from Step 4.

6 Narrow-hem (page 11) the bottom edge of the skirt (the seventh band). Run two rows of gathering stitches along the top edge of the skirt. (See pages 11–12 for how to gather and for measuring, marking and gathering the skirt to the bottom of the polo shirt.)

7 If desired, make a hair tie and/or a sash (see page 15). ✲

34

Quilting Bee

We used fat quarters to make the patchwork yardage for the skirt of this folksy frock, but you can also use charm packs, jelly rolls, or your fabric stash.

A variety of colors can create a beautiful patchwork

What You'll Need:

● Basic tool kit (page 7)

● T-shirt

● For the skirt: 10 (10, 12, 12) fat quarters

● 2 packages jumbo rickrack

Instructions are for sizes Small (Medium, Large, Extra-Large). Sample shown in size Small. Patchwork seam allowances are ¼", all other seam allowances are ½" unless otherwise noted.

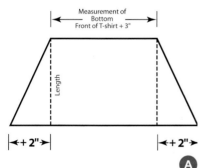

Getting Ready

1 Lay the T-shirt out flat, measure and mark 2" (2½", 3", 3¼") down from each underarm seam, and follow the cutting instructions on page 6. Mark the center front and center back of the shirt.

2 Measure across the front of the shirt from seam to seam at the bottom edge and add 3"; this measurement is for the top edge of each skirt piece (front and back). Add 4" to the skirt top edge measurement for the bottom (hem) measurement (see Figure A). This creates a slight A-line silhouette and provides walking ease. Create two pieces of patchwork fabric (see Steps 4–6) to this width measurement and the length measurement indicated in the following chart.

	S (2/3)	M (4/5)	L (6/6x)	XL (7/8)
Skirt length	12"	13"	13½"	14"

3 For the ruffle, determine the hem circumference of the skirt and multiply by 2 for the width measurement. The cutting length is 4" for a finished length of 3". Cut enough 4" long ruffle pieces from one or two fat quarters to make the desired width ruffle.

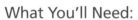

Quilting Bee

Making the Patchwork

4 From the remaining fat quarters, cut enough 2½" squares to make a skirt front and skirt back to the desired measurements (see Step 2 above). (If you want to line the dress, take care to cut the squares so you'll have several larger pieces that you can use as a lining.) For example, for a skirt front measuring 16" wide by 12" long, you would need to cut at least 48 squares (16 ÷ 2 = 8 squares across, by 12 ÷ 2 = 6 squares long). Note that if you want to use the patchwork on the diagonal (as shown in the sample), you'll need to cut additional squares.

5 Before sewing the squares, arrange all of them in rows to make sure you like the pattern. Starting with the top row, sew the squares into strips with right sides together and ¼" seams. Press the seams open or to one side. Then sew all the strips together, aligning seams, and press. Sew enough strips together to make two pieces of patchwork fabric large enough to cut the skirt front and back.

6 Trim the patchwork fabric to the measurements for the skirt front and back and sew them with right sides together at the side seams. If you want to line the dress, sew the remaining fabric together to the same measurements as the skirt front and back and sew the side seams. Pin the wrong side of the lining to the wrong side of the patchwork and baste the top edges together.

Sewing the Dress

7 Stitch the ruffle pieces with right sides together to form a circle, press the seams, and narrow-hem (see page 11) the bottom edge. Stitch rickrack to the bottom edge of the ruffle so it peeks outs below the hemmed edge. Set the ruffle aside.

8 Mark the center front and center back of the skirt and pin the top edge to the bottom edge of the T-shirt, stretching the T-shirt slightly to fit the skirt. Sew the layers together, treating the patchwork and lining as one. Press.

9 Topstitch the rickrack directly over the seam, starting at one side seam and overlapping the ends of the rickrack. Stitch directly through the center of the rickrack.

10 Measure and mark the top edge of the ruffle in quarters (see page 13). Run two rows of gathering stitches along the top edge of the ruffle (see pages 11–12 for how to gather). Pull the gathering stitches and pin the ruffle to the bottom of the patchwork with right sides together and the markings aligned with the center front, center back, and sides seams of the skirt. Adjust the gathers so they're evenly distributed and stitch. Press.❈

Square Dance

This fun look is made with three bandannas: two for layering over a checked skirt and one for the sash. Create a playful palette by using bandannas in contrasting colors.

Do-si-do and swing your partner . . . promenade!

What You'll Need:

- Basic tool kit (page 7)
- T-shirt
- For the skirt and flower: ½ yard 45"-wide fabric
- To embellish the skirt: 3 bandannas, each 21" square
- Pin back

Instructions are for sizes Small (Medium, Large, Extra-Large). Sample shown in size Large. All seam allowances are ½" unless otherwise noted.

Getting Ready

1 Lay the T-shirt out flat, measure and mark 4½" (4¾", 5", 5½") down from each underarm seam, and follow the cutting instructions on page 6. Mark the center front and center back of the shirt.

2 Measure the circumference at the bottom edge of the T-shirt and multiply by 1.5 to determine the cutting width for the skirt fabric. Refer to the chart below for the length measurements.

	S (2/3)	M (4/5)	L (6/6x)	XL (7/8)
Skirt length	11"	13"	15"	16"

Sewing the Dress

3 Narrow-hem (see page 11) one long edge of the skirt fabric. With right sides together, sew the shorter edges of the skirt to form a circle; the seam will be the center back of the skirt. Measure and mark the center front and sides of the skirt (see page 12).

4 With right sides up, place a bandanna on the center front of the skirt so the bottom edge of the bandanna is about 2" above the bottom edge of the skirt; pin in place. Repeat to position and pin another bandanna on the center back of the skirt. Cut off the excess bandanna above the upper edge of the skirt. Baste the edges together.

Square Dance

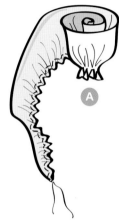

A

5 Sew two rows of basting stitches along the top edge of the skirt (through both layers), one on each side of the first row of basting stitches from Step 4.

6 Pull the basting stitches so the skirt fits the bottom edge of the T-shirt, matching markings and adjusting the gathers so the bandannas are centered in the front and back of the skirt (see pages 11–12 for how to gather). Stitch.

7 Cut the remaining bandanna into three 3"-wide strips. Sew the strips together along short ends to make one long strip for the sash. Clean-finish the edges as for a single-layer sash (see page 15).

8 To make a flower (optional), cut a strip of skirt fabric 3" wide and 12" long and a 2¼"-diameter circle. Fold the strip in half lengthwise, wrong sides together, and run two rows of gathering stitches along the cut edges. Pull the gathers so they're tight and knot the thread ends. Starting at one end, roll the strip to form the flower, hand-stitching the bottom edges together as you roll (see Figure A). Zigzag around the perimeter of the circle, then hand-sew it to cover the gathered edges and create a stay. Sew a pin back to the stay. Pin it to the sash or T-shirt. ✷

Flower Girl

Take a simple T-shirt or tank top, add a lined chiffon skirt, stir in eyelet trim and flowers with pearl accents, and voilà—little-girl elegance.

A lovely look for a casual spring wedding or summer party

What You'll Need:

- Basic tool kit (page 7)
- T-shirt or tank top
- ¾ yard 60"-wide chiffon
- ¾ yard 60"-wide satin or other lining fabric
- For the waist and flowers: 3 yards 1"-wide pregathered eyelet trim
- For the hem: 1¾ yards 2½"-wide trim
- Small sew-on pearls (one for each flower)

Instructions are for sizes Small (Medium, Large, Extra-Large). Sample shown in size Medium. All seam allowances are ½" unless otherwise noted.

Getting Ready

1 Lay the T-shirt out flat, measure and mark 3¾" (4", 4½", 4½") down from each underarm seam, and follow the cutting instructions on page 6. Mark the center front and center back of the shirt.

2 Cut the lining fabric and the chiffon overskirt fabric the same size. For the fabric width, use one width of fabric for each (for a fuller skirt, cut two fabric widths and seam them together—you'll need more fabric). Refer to the chart below for the length measurements.

	S (2/3)	M (4/5)	L (6/6x)	XL (7/8)
Skirt length	20"	22"	23"	24"

Sewing the Dress

3 With the right sides together, sew the center back seams of the overskirt and lining. Clean-finish or zigzag the seam allowances to prevent raveling.

4 Narrow-hem (see page 11, Method 3) each skirt bottom edge. Slide the wrong side of the overskirt over the right side of the lining skirt and baste the top edges together.

Flower Girl

5 Run two rows of basting stitches along the top edge, one on either side of the basting from Step 4 (see pages 11–12 for how to gather). With the seam at the center back, measure and mark the center front and sides (page 12).

6 With right sides and straight edges together, pin the pre-gathered narrow eyelet trim to the bottom edge of the T-shirt, then baste it in place.

7 Pull the gathering threads on the skirt so the markings on the skirt and bottom of the T-shirt align. Adjust the gathers and pin the layers with right sides together and the eyelet sandwiched between. Stitch, then zigzag the seam allowances.

8 Machine-stitch the wider eyelet trim to the bottom edge of the lining fabric.

9 To make an eyelet flower, cut an 8"-long piece of the narrow eyelet trim (A). Run a line of gathering stitches just inside the binding edge (in the eyelet) and knot one end (B). Pull the gathers so the eyelet forms a tight circle and pin it to hold it tight. Zigzag randomly over the center, catching the edges of the eyelet to hold the circle in place (C). Handstitch a pearl in the center (D). Repeat to make as many eyelet flowers as desired. Sew them to the dress. ✳

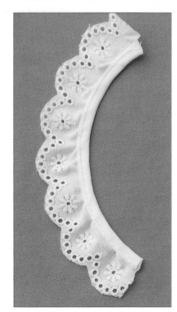

A

B   C   D

It's a Wrap

This fuss-free design makes getting dressed in the morning a cinch—she'll be ready in no time and excited to start her busy day.

Smart, yet casual—definitely dressed for success

What You'll Need:

- Basic tool kit (page 7)
- T-shirt
- For the skirt, front wrap, and ties: ¾ yard (¾ yard, 1 yard, 1 yard) 45"-wide fabric
- 1 package mini pompom trim
- Zipper foot
- For the flower (optional): fabric scraps, 3 individual mini pompoms, pin back

Instructions are for sizes Small (Medium, Large, Extra-Large). Sample shown in size Small. All seam allowances are ½" unless otherwise noted.

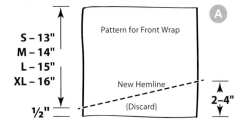

S – 13"
M – 14"
L – 15"
XL – 16"

½"

Pattern for Front Wrap

New Hemline

{Discard}

A

2–4"

Getting Ready

1 Lay the T-shirt out flat, measure and mark 4½" (5½", 6", 6½") down from each underarm seam, and follow the cutting instructions on page 6. Mark the center front and center back of the shirt.

2 Measure the circumference at the bottom edge of the T-shirt and multiply by 1.25. Divide this number by 2 to determine the width of the skirt front and the skirt back. Refer to the chart below for the cutting length for each size, then cut a skirt front and skirt back.

	S (2/3)	M (4/5)	L (6/6x)	XL (7/8)
Skirt length	13"	14"	15"	16"

3 For the front wrap section, make a paper pattern or draw the following measurements with a fabric marker or chalk directly on the fabric, adjusting measurements as desired (see Figure A).

Width: Measure the width of the skirt front as cut; subtract between 5" (for Small and Medium) to 8" (for Large and Extra-Large).
Length: Measure the length of the skirt front as cut; subtract ½" on the left side and between 2" to 4" on the right side.

4 For the ties, cut two 30" x 6" pieces.

It's a Wrap

Sewing the Dress

5 Press the shorter side and the bottom edge of the front wrap piece ½" to the wrong side. Using the zipper foot, sew the pompom trim to the wrong side of the folded edge, pivoting the stitching at the corner.

6 With right sides up, place the wrap piece over the skirt front, aligning the left and upper edges; baste (the layers will be treated as one in following steps). With right sides together, pin the skirt front to the back along the sides; stitch. Mark the center front and center back of the skirt.

7 Narrow-hem (see page 11) the bottom of the skirt.

8 Gather the upper edge of skirt (see pages 11–12 for how to gather). Pin the gathered edge to the lower edge of the T-shirt, aligning marks and seams. Adjust the gathers and stitch the skirt to shirt. Press seams toward the shirt. Remove visible basting stitches.

9 To make each tie, fold the 30" x 6" strip in half lengthwise with right sides together. Cut one short end diagonally. Stitch the long and diagonal edges (see Figure B). Trim seam allowances and corners; turn right side out. Press. Clean-finish the open edge and press it ½" to one side.

Fold

B

10 Pin the folded edge of each tie end at each side seam, centered over the waist seam; edgestitch in place.

11 To make a flower (optional), cut a piece of skirt fabric 3" wide x 8" long. Fold the strip in half lengthwise, wrong sides together, and finish the cut edges with a zigzag stitch. Run a row of gathering stitches along the sewn edge, then pull them to tighten, creating a flattened circle. Position as much of the stitching at the back of the flower as possible. Overlap the two short ends at the back of the flower and hand-sew to create a stay. Sew three mini pompoms in the center. Attach a pin back.

Ship-shape

Give a T-shirt a nautical touch by adding a drawstring to the bottom edge, and suddenly you have a great summer dress.

Set sail in fresh stripes and geometric prints

What You'll Need:

- Basic tool kit (page 7)
- T-shirt or tank top
- For the top band: ¼ yard 45"-wide fabric
- For the bottom band and pocket: ⅓ yard 45"-wide fabric
- For the bottom binding: ⅛ yard 45"-wide fabric
- Pocket template (page 17)
- 1¼ yards cotton cording or other drawstring
- 2" x 2" scrap of fusible interfacing
- 1 package double-fold, double-wide bias binding
- Safety pin

Instructions are for sizes Small (Medium, Large, Extra-Large). Sample shown in size Large. All seam allowances are ½" unless otherwise noted.

Getting Ready

1 Cut off the bottom hem of the T-shirt.

2 Measure the circumference at the bottom edge of the T-shirt and multiply by 1½ to determine the width of each piece. Refer to the chart below for the length measurements.

	S (2/3)	M (4/5)	L (6/6x)	XL (7/8)
Top band	4½"	5½"	6"	6½"
Bottom band	5"	6"	6½"	7"
Bottom binding	2"	2"	2"	2"

3 Using the template (see page 17), cut two pockets.

Sewing the Dress

4 With right sides together, sew the pocket pieces together, leaving a small opening on one side for turning. Trim the seam allowances and turn the pocket right side out. Press the pocket and press the seam allowances at the opening to the inside. Sew two rows of topstitching 1" from the top edge. Pin the pocket to the front of the T-shirt and edgestitch the sides and bottom edges in place.

Ship-shape

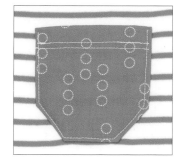

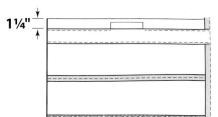

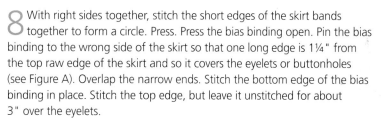

5 With the right sides together, sew the top band to the bottom band along one long edge. Press the seam toward the bottom band. With right sides together, stitch the bottom binding to the lower edge of the bottom band. Press the seam toward the bottom binding. Press the remaining long edge of the bottom binding ¼" to the wrong side. Press the folded edge of the bottom binding up and over to cover the seam on the wrong side. Edgestitch the bottom binding in place.

6 Fold the stitched bands in half, then in quarters, lengthwise, and mark the top edge at the halfway and quarter marks with chalk or pins. Fold the T-shirt in half to mark the center of the front and back along the bottom edge.

7 Following the manufacturer's instructions, fuse the interfacing to the wrong side of the skirt front ½" from the top edge at the center marking. Make two small eyelets or buttonholes on the interfacing 1½" below the top edge and ½" apart. Clip the buttonholes or eyelets open.

8 With right sides together, stitch the short edges of the skirt bands together to form a circle. Press. Press the bias binding open. Pin the bias binding to the wrong side of the skirt so that one long edge is 1¼" from the top raw edge of the skirt and so it covers the eyelets or buttonholes (see Figure A). Overlap the narrow ends. Stitch the bottom edge of the bias binding in place. Stitch the top edge, but leave it unstitched for about 3" over the eyelets.

9 Attach the safety pin to one end of the cording to make a drawstring. From the right side insert the cording into one eyelet, then run it through the casing all the way around the skirt to the other eyelet. Draw it through the remaining eyelet from the wrong side to the right side. Knot both ends of the drawstring. Stitch the opening in the top edge of the bias binding closed, taking care to avoid stitching through the cording.

10 Run two rows of gathering stitches between the top edge of the skirt and the casing (see pages 11–12 for how to gather). Pull the stitches slightly to gather the skirt to the bottom edge of the T-shirt. With right sides together, pin the T-shirt and skirt together, adjusting the gathers so the seams and markings align. Make sure the eyelets are in the front of the T-shirt. Stitch; remove the gathering stitches if they're visible. Press.✳

❋ ❋ ❋ ❋

Flirty Shirt

Take the "T-shirt and jeans" look to a new level. Alter a T-shirt with a tunic-length skirt made with bright print fabrics, then use the remnants to upscale plain jeans.

Perfect for your flower child or twirly dancer

What You'll Need:

● Basic tool kit (page 7)

● T-shirt

● For the skirt panels, sash, and kerchief: see the yardage chart (right)

● For the kerchief trim: 1 yard pre-gathered 1" trim

● For the kerchief ties: 1 yard narrow ribbon

● Double-sided, paper-backed fusible web

● Denim jeans

Instructions are for sizes Small (Medium, Large, Extra-Large). Sample shown in size Medium. All seam allowances are ½" unless otherwise noted.

45"-wide fabric	S (2/3)	M (4/5)	L (6/6x)	XL (7/8)
Fabric 1 (skirt panels, sash, kerchief)	⅔ yard	⅔ yard	⅔ yard	1 yard
Fabric 2 (skirt panels)	½ yard	½ yard	½ yard	½ yard

Getting Ready

1 Lay the T-shirt out flat, measure and mark 1½" (1¾", 2", 2½") down from each underarm seam, and follow the cutting instructions on page 6. Mark the center front and center back of the shirt.

2 Using Figure A as a guide, cut six fabric panels for the tunic skirt from each fabric as follows:

	S (2/3)	M (4/5)	L (6/6x)	XL (7/8)
Each panel	6¼" x 13"	6½" x 13½"	6¾" x 14"	7" x 15"

(A) For the sash, cut one piece 5" x 44". For the kerchief, cut out a 14" square of Fabric 1; set aside.

44"

2"

|←3"→|
OPENING

←2"→   ←2"→

B

❋ ❋ ❋ ❋

Flirty Shirt

C

Sewing the Dress

3 Alternating fabrics and with right sides together, sew all the panels together along the long sides to form a tube. Press the seam allowances open.

4 Narrow-hem (page 11) one edge of the joined panels. Mark the bottom of the T-shirt and top of the skirt. Gather the unfinished edge of the skirt and sew the layers together (see pages 11–12).

Sewing the Sash

5 Fold the sash piece with the right sides together and stitch all three open sides, leaving a 3"-inch opening for turning. Stitch the ends at an angle as shown (see Figure B). Trim the ends. Turn the sash right side out. Press the seam allowances at the opening to the inside and slipstitch the opening closed. Press again.

Sewing the Kerchief

6 Press all edges on the 14" square of fabric ½" to the wrong side, then press the square in half diagonally, wrong sides together, to form a triangle.

7 Cut the ribbon into two 18" pieces. Place one end just inside each pressed edge, near the fold, and tack them in place.

8 Pin the trim between the pressed edges of the kerchief (fold the cut edges of the trim to one side before pinning). Edgestitch through all the layers to sew the kerchief, catching the edge of the trim and the ends of the ribbon ties in the seam (see Figure C).

Appliquéing the Jeans

9 Rough cut several motifs from fabric scraps, allowing a 2" perimeter all around each motif.

10 Following the manufacturer's instructions, apply the fusible web to the rough-cut appliqué fabric. Cut out the motifs exactly as you want them to appear. Remove the backing paper and fuse the motif(s) onto the jeans. If desired, satin stitch around the outside edge of the motifs.❋

Oo-La-La

Alternate layers of tulle and cotton-print ruffles to make an adorable little dress with lots of personality.

What You'll Need:
- Basic tool kit (page 7)
- T-shirt
- Fabrics for the skirt: see the yardage chart (right)
- Tulle for the skirt: 2 rolls 6"-wide precut tulle in two colors
- For the bow: ½ yard of ¾"-wide ribbon

Instructions are for sizes Small (Medium, Large, Extra-Large). Sample shown in size Small. All seam allowances are ½" unless otherwise noted.

A sweet bow is the finishing touch

45"-wide fabric	S (2/3) / M (4/5)	L (6/6x) / XL (7/8)
Top ruffle	¼ yard	⅓ yard
Bottom ruffle	¼ yard	½ yard

Getting Ready

1 Lay the T-shirt out flat, measure and mark 7½" (7½", 8½", 8½") down from each underarm seam and follow the cutting instructions on page 6. Mark the center front and center back of the shirt.

2 Measure the bottom edge of the cut T-shirt and multiply by 2 to determine the cutting width of the fabric ruffles. Cut and stitch two pieces together if needed to achieve the correct width.

For the top tulle ruffle: Cut two 45" pieces and baste together at one long edge.
For the bottom tulle ruffle: Cut one 90" piece

See the chart below for the cutting lengths for all the ruffles, which are the same for all sizes. The dress will be shorter on a taller child, but you can adjust the length of the ruffles to suit.

Top fabric ruffle: 5½" long
Top tulle ruffle: 4½" long

Bottom fabric ruffle: 8" long
Bottom tulle ruffle: 6" long

> **✳ TIP**
> If the T-shirt measurement is close to 45", simply use one fabric width.

Oo-La-La

Sewing the Dress

3 Narrow-hem (see page 11) one long edge of each of the fabric ruffles.

4 Run one row of gathering stitches across the top of the lower tulle ruffle (see pages 11–12 for how to gather) and pull the stitching to gather the tulle to fit the lower fabric ruffle. Pin the gathered edge of the tulle to the right side of the bottom ruffle so that the bottom edge of the tulle is about 1" above the hemmed edge of the ruffle, then baste the top edge in place. (Note that the top edge of the tulle should not reach the top edge of the fabric ruffle.)

5 Layer the wrong side of the top fabric ruffle over the right side of the bottom tulle ruffle so the top edges of the fabric ruffles align. Layer the double layers of the top tulle ruffle (gathering them as needed to fit the top ruffle) on top, then baste all the layers together.

6 With right sides together, sew the short ends of the ruffles together to make the center back seam. Stitch through all the layers.

7 Run two rows of gathering stitches along the top edge through all the layers. Measure and mark the top edge of the skirt and the bottom edge of the T-shirt (see page 12). Pull the gathers to fit the skirt and T-shirt and pin them with right sides together and markings aligned. Adjust the gathers and stitch.

8 To make the fabric trim shown between the skirt and the T-shirt, cut two pieces of either fabric 1½" wide by the desired length of the trim multiplied by 2 (see page 13 for how to make a double ruffle). Lay the trim right side up over the seam and pull the gathering stitches so the trim fits around the skirt and the gathers are evenly distributed. Topstitch the trim to the dress.

9 Tie a ribbon bow and handstitch it in place.✷

Summer Breeze

It's hard to believe this sundress starts as a basic T-shirt. With the neckline ties it's easy to fit and easy to wear for all kinds of summer fun.

Cool fun in the summertime

What You'll Need:

- Basic tool kit (page 7)
- T-shirt
- For the skirt: ½ yard 45"-wide fabric
- For the bottom band and neckline tie: ½ yard 45"-wide fabric
- For the ruffle and armhole binding: ¼ yard 45"-wide fabric
- Safety pin

Instructions are for sizes Small (Medium, Large, Extra-Large). Sample shown in size Extra-Large. All seam allowances are ½" unless otherwise noted.

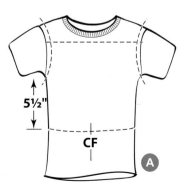

5½"

CF

A

Getting Ready

1 Lay the T-shirt out flat. Draw a line straight across the top of the shirt just below the neckline. Measure and mark 5" (5½", 6", 6½") down from each underarm seam and draw a line across the T-shirt connecting the markings. Cut the T-shirt across the two horizontal marked lines, then cut away the sleeves and the sleeve seams. Mark the center front and center back of the shirt (see Figure A).

2 Use one entire width of the fabric, approximately 45", for the width of the skirt and the bottom band. Use two fabric widths (90") for the ruffle. Refer to the chart below for the cutting length of the skirt, ruffle, and band.

	S (2/3)	M (4/5)	L (6/6x)	XL (7/8)
Skirt length	12"	13"	13½"	14"
Ruffle length	2"	2"	2"	2"
Band length	3"	3"	4"	4"

3 For the neckline drawstring, cut two 2"-wide strips across the width of the fabric. Stitch two short ends together to make one long drawstring. (The drawstring will be trimmed to the correct length after trying the dress on the child.)

�֍ �֍ ✖ ✖

Peachy Keen

9 Cut another piece of ribbon equal in length to the back bottom edge of the shirt + 1". Press it in half, then press the narrow edges ½" to the wrong side. Pin the ribbon to the back of the dress from side seam to side seam, covering the top, raw edge of the skirt and the seamline. Edgestitch the ribbon in place along both long edges.

10 Pin the lower edge of the waistband directly over the front shirt/skirt seam (the upper edge of the waistband will fall along the other marked placement line drawn in step 1) and edgestitch the waistband to the shirt, stitching along the folded and side edges of the ribbon. The sashes are not stitched down.

11 To make a bow (optional), cut three pieces of fabric as follows:

Lower loop: 10" x 4"
Upper loop: 8" x 2"
Knot: 2" x 3"

Fold each piece in half lengthwise with right sides together and stitch only the long edge. Turn the pieces right side out and press so the seam is in the center of each piece.

12 Mark the center of each loop and fold the raw edges to meet at the marking. Zigzag or hand-stitch them in place (see Figure C).

13 Position the smaller loos over the longer loop and tack them together with several hand stitches. Wrap the knot (with the seam on the bottom) around the loops, pulling the knot piece tight to shape the bow. Overlap the ends of the knot underneath the bow and trim excess fabric if needed; Handstitch the ends together. Handstitch the bow to the dress or to a pin backing.✖

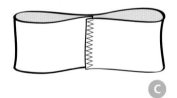

C

Swirly Girl

The long, uneven hemline of this sweet dress makes it perfect for a little girl who wants to twirl her summer days away!

Take a spin in a pretty summer garden

You'll Need:

- Basic tool kit (page 7)
- Yardstick
- T-shirt
- 1¾ yards of 45"-wide fabric for the skirt and hem band lining
- ¾ yard of 45"-wide fabric for the hem band and flower

Instructions are for sizes Small (Medium, Large, Extra-Large). Sample shown in size Small. All seam allowances are ½" unless otherwise noted.

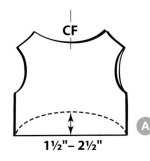

Getting Ready

1 Lay the T-shirt out flat, measure and mark 4" (for Small and Medium) or 5" (for Large and Extra-Large) down from each underarm seam, and follow the cutting instructions on page 6. Mark the center front and center back of the shirt. At the center front and center back, measure 1½" (for Small and Medium) or 2½" (for Large and Extra-Large) up from the bottom of the shirt and mark. On the front of the shirt, draw a gently shaped curve from the side seam to the center marking and back to the other side seam. Fold the shirt in half at the center and adjust the lines to make them symmetrical. Repeat on the back of the shirt. Cut along the marked lines (see Figure A). Set aside the bottom of the shirt to make the neckline ruffle.

2 Press the skirt fabric open. Then fold it in half widthwise. With a yardstick and fabric marker or chalk, mark and cut a trapezoid shape (through both layers of folded fabric) for the front and back skirt as described below.

	S (2/3)/M(4/5)	L (6/6x)/XL(7/8)
Width at top	20"	30"
Width at bottom	30"	40"
Length	16"	19"

3 To shape the two skirt pieces, draw top and bottom cutting lines as shown in the two skirt drawings (see Figures B and C on page 66). Draw lines to mark the center front and center back first, then the shaped lines. Cut the front and back skirt pieces along the shaped design lines.

Swirly Girl

4 Cut one front and one back hem band from the hem band fabric and one front and one back hem band from the skirt fabric to act as a lining (the back bands are longer). Follow the cutting measurements in the chart below, then draw the shaped cutting lines as indicated in Figures D and E on page 66. The front piece is only shaped along the top edge; the back piece is shaped both top and bottom.

	S (2/3)/M(4/5)	L (6/6x)/XL(7/8)
Front hem band		
Width at top	40"	55"
Width at bottom	60"	70"
Length	8"	9"
Back hem band		
Width at top	40"	55"
Width at bottom	60"	70"
Length	10"	12"

Sewing the Dress

5 With right sides together, sew the front skirt and back skirt together and the hem band (front and back) and hem band lining pieces together to form circles. Because of the shaping, you may need to cut off some of the bottom edge of the pieces at the side seams.

6 With right sides together, stitch the hem band and hem band lining together along the bottom edge. Turn the pieces right side out (wrong sides together) and press. Edgestitch around the hem edge. Baste the top edges together.

7 Run two rows of gathering stitches along the top edge of the skirt and the two-layer hem band. Mark the centers and sides of all the pieces. Pull the gathering stitches on the hem band and pin, adjust, and sew it to the bottom edge of the skirt (see page 12). Repeat to sew the top of the skirt to the bottom of the shirt.

8 Measure the front neckline of the shirt and multiply by 2. Cut a piece of fabric from the bottom of the T-shirt to that measurement by 1½" wide, stitching two pieces together if needed to achieve the correct measurement. Make a double ruffle (see page 13) and stitch it to the neckline of the shirt.

9 Make a flower with fabric remnants (see page 40, Step 8). The rose shown is made from a strip of fabric 3" x 18". ✸

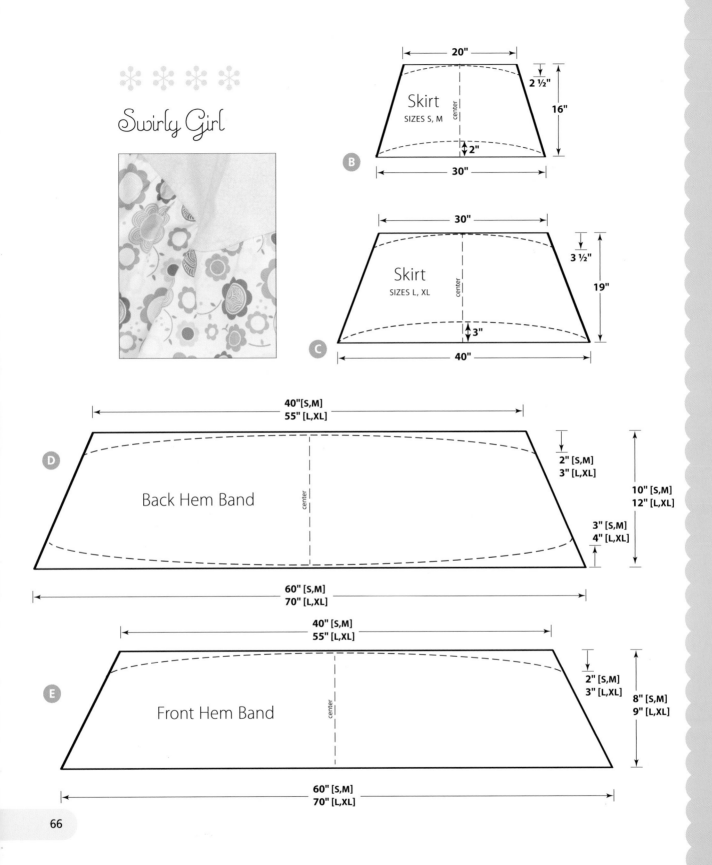

Swirly Girl

B Skirt
SIZES S, M

20"
2 ½"
16"
center
2"
30"

C Skirt
SIZES L, XL

30"
3 ½"
19"
center
3"
40"

D Back Hem Band

40"[S,M]
55" [L,XL]

2" [S,M]
3" [L,XL]

10" [S,M]
12" [L,XL]

3" [S,M]
4" [L,XL]

center

60" [S,M]
70" [L,XL]

E Front Hem Band

40" [S,M]
55" [L,XL]

2" [S,M]
3" [L,XL]

8" [S,M]
9" [L,XL]

center

60" [S,M]
70" [L,XL]

Tea Party

It's more than charming fabric—the elegant scalloped edge and the straight, fit-and-flare silhouette make this a perfect dress for tea parties and playdates.

"Tip me over and pour me out!"

What You'll Need:

- Basic tool kit (page 7)
- T-shirt or tank top
- For the dress: ½ yard 45"-wide fabric
- For the ruffle: ½ yard 45"-wide fabric
- Scalloped edge template (see page 17)
- Lightweight cardboard
- 1 package piping
- Zipper foot
- For the scalloped flower (optional): 1 button and pin back

Instructions are for sizes Small (Medium, Large, Extra-Large). Sample shown in size Small. All seam allowances are ½" unless otherwise noted.

Getting Ready

1 Lay the T-shirt out flat, measure and mark 2" (2½", 3", 3½") down from each underarm seam, and follow the cutting instructions on page 6. Set aside the bottom of the T-shirt. Mark the center front and center back of the shirt.

2 Measure the circumference of the bottom edge of the T-shirt and add 5" (for a straighter silhouette) to 10" (for a fuller silhouette) for the cutting width of the dress fabric. For the ruffle, multiply the measurement of the dress fabric (which you just determined by choosing the flair of the silhouette) by 3. Refer to the chart below for the cutting length of the dress and the ruffle.

	S (2/3)	M (4/5)	L (6/6x)	XL (7/8)
Dress	10"	11"	12"	13"
Ruffle	6"	6½"	7"	8"

Sewing the Dress

3 Cut the hem off the bottom section of the T-shirt. To make the lining for the scalloped edge, cut a 2"-wide strip from the bottom of the shirt, leaving the side seams intact to make a circle.

4 Trace the scalloped edge template (see page 17) onto lightweight cardboard, then cut it out.

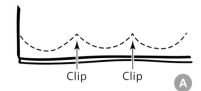

Tea Party

Clip   Clip

5 On the *wrong* side of the T-shirt, position the template so the bottom of the scallops are ¼" above the cut edge of the T-shirt, then trace the template with a fabric marking pen or chalk. Continue, tracing the scallops onto both the front and the back of the T-shirt, repositioning the template along the cut edge as needed.

6 With right sides together, stitch the lining for the scalloped edge (from Step 3) to the bottom edge of the T-shirt along the marked line, pivoting at curves. Trim the seam allowance and clip into the inside points (see Figure A).

7 Turn the facing to the wrong side of the T-shirt and steam-press the scalloped edge, taking care not to stretch the scallops.

8 Hand-baste the piping along the scalloped edge, overlapping the ends at one side seam. Trim the facing on the inside of the T-shirt to 1" wide.

9 With right sides together, stitch the center back seam of the dress and mark the center front and sides (see page 12). Run two rows of gathering stitches around the top edge (see pages 11–12 for how to gather).

10 Make the ruffle by sewing all the cut pieces with the right sides together at the short edges to form a circle. Narrow-hem (see page 11) the bottom edge. Run two rows of gathering stitches along the top edge.

11 With right sides together, pin the ruffle to the bottom edge of the dress, pulling the gathering stitches on the ruffle so it fits the dress and the markings align. Stitch.

12 Pull the gathering stitches on the top edge of the dress. Position the top edge of the dress (right-side up) under the scalloped edge of the T-shirt so the scallops cover the gathering stitches. Align the centers and side seam markings, and make sure none of the gathering stitches are visible. Pin the layers together. Install zipper foot. Edgestitch the T-shirt along the scalloped edge, using the basting stitches from Step 8 as a guide (see Figure B).

13 To make a flower (optional), use the scalloped edge template (see page 17) to cut two strips of dress fabric 2" x 22". Sew the two pieces together along one long edge. Trim and clip as in Step 6. Turn the scalloped strip right side out and press. Zigzag or overlock the open edges (one long and both short) together. Run a row of gathering stitches along the long, straight edge. Pull the threads to gather the strip into a flower. Sew a button over the center. Sew the pin back to the flower.✻

Fringe Benefits

This tunic-length top features a skirt made with two tiers of lightweight chambray embellished with decorative fringe created from fabric and ribbon.

This tunic keeps tabs on style

What You'll Need:

● Basic tool kit (page 7)

● T-shirt

● For the tunic skirt: ½ yard 45"-wide lightweight chambray or denim

● For the decorative tabs: charm pack, fabric remnants, and/or assorted ribbons

● Embroidery thread (in a color that contrasts with the chambray and matches the T-shirt and tabs)

● 1 package jumbo rickrack

Instructions are for sizes Small (Medium, Large, Extra-Large). Sample shown in size Extra-Large.
All seam allowances are ½" unless otherwise noted.

Getting Ready

1 Lay the T-shirt out flat, measure and mark 6" (6¼", 6½", 7") down from each underarm seam, and follow the cutting instructions on page 6.

2 To determine the cutting width and length for each tier, measure the circumference of the bottom of the shirt and refer to Figure A and the chart below. The tiers should be slightly wider across the bottom edge so they flare slightly and the top tier fits smoothly over the bottom tier.

Cutting widths

Top tier: measurement + 2" at top edge; + 5" at bottom edge
Bottom tier: measurement + 1½" at top edge; + 5" at bottom edge

Cutting lengths

	S (2/3)	M (4/5)	L (6/6x)	XL (7/8)
Top tier	4"	5"	5½"	6"
Bottom tier	8"	8½"	9"	9½"

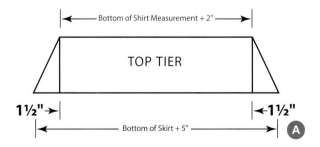

❄ ❄ ❄ ❄

Bubble Tee

A bubble hemline is easy to sew—a sweet silhouette that'll make her look like she's floating on air.

Spot on for a bubbly personality

What You'll Need:

- Basic tool kit (page 7)
- T-shirt or tank top
- For the skirt: 1 yard 45"-wide fabric
- For the lining: ½ yard 45"-wide fabric
- 1 yard pompom fringe
- Zipper foot

Instructions are for sizes Small (Medium, Large, Extra-Large). Sample shown in size Small. All seam allowances are ½" unless otherwise noted.

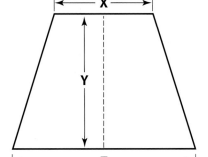

Getting Ready

1 Lay the T-shirt out flat, measure and mark 3" (3½", 4½", 4½") down from each each underarm seam, and follow the cutting instructions on page 6. Mark the center front and center back of the shirt.

2 For the skirt, measure the cut edge of the T-shirt from seam to seam, then multiply this measurement by 2 to calculate the cutting width of each piece (front and back). Refer to the chart below for the cutting length.

	S (2/3)	M (4/5)	L (6/6x)	XL (7/8)
Length of skirt pieces (cut 2)	14"	15"	16"	18"

3 For the lining, cut two pieces (front and back) using the seam-to-seam measurement of the bottom of the T-shirt and Figure A as a guide. The trapezoid shape of the lining supports the bubble shape of the skirt.

X (top edge) = seam-to-seam measurement + 2"
Y (same as for skirt) = cutting length
Z (bottom edge) = seam-to-seam measurement + 5"

Sewing the Dress

4 With right sides together, sew the short edges of the skirt pieces together to make a circle. Form a circle from the lining pieces in the same way. Run two rows of gathering stitches around the top and bottom edges of the skirt and (see pages 11–12 for how to gather).

Bubble Tee

5 With right sides together, pin the bottom edges of the skirt and the lining together, aligning the side seams and adjusting gathers so the skirt gathers are evenly distributed. Stitch the skirt and the lining together at the bottom edge.

6 Fold the lining to the inside of the skirt so the wrong sides are together and the top edges are aligned. Pull the basting stitches on the top of the skirt to gather it to fit the lining. With the side seams aligned, baste the edges together.

7 Pin the trim to the bottom edge of the T-shirt so the header is within the seam allowance. Attach the zipper foot to the machine and baste the trim in place at the base of the header.

8 With right sides together and the trim sandwiched between them, pin the bottom edge of the T-shirt to the top edge of the skirt. Stitch, stretching the T-shirt slightly to fit the skirt.✳

❋ ❋ ❋ ❋

Uptown Girl

This little dress, inspired by the timeless Chanel suit, is so easy to sew it'll be "ready to wear" in no time.

What You'll Need:

● Basic tool kit (page 7)

● Press cloth

For Dress 1 (black top):

● Black T-shirt

● For the skirt: see yardage chart (right)

● For the pockets: 24" x 24" remnant of black fabric

● For the trim: ¼ yard 45"-wide sequined fabric and 4 to 5 buttons

For Dress 2 (white top; see page 82):

● White T-shirt

● For the skirt: see yardage chart (right)

● For the pockets: 24" x 24" remnant of white fabric

● For the trim: 2 yards 1"-wide elastic sequin trim, 1½ yards ⅜"-wide elastic sequin trim, and 4 to 5 buttons

Instructions are for sizes Small (Medium, Large, Extra-Large). Sample shown in size Large. All seam allowances are ½" unless otherwise noted.

Start with a simple tee—finish with great style

45"-wide fabric	S (2/3) / M (4/5)	L (6/6x) / XL (7/8)
	¾ yard	1 yard

Getting Ready

1 Lay the T-shirt out flat and cut off the bottom hem. Turn the raw edge ¼" to the wrong side and zigzag the folded edge. Mark the center front and center back of the shirt.

2 Measure the circumference at the bottom edge of the T-shirt and multiply by 3 to determine the fabric cutting width for the skirt. Refer to the chart below for the length measurements.

	S (2/3)	M (4/5)	L (6/6x)	XL (7/8)
Skirt fabric length	12"	14"	15"	15½"

3 For the pockets, cut four 5" squares from the remnant fabric.

✳ ✳ ✳ ✳

Uptown Girl

Embellishing the Top

Note: The black dress features sequined fabric and the white dress features elastic sequin trim. The instructions below are for preparing and attaching sequined *fabric*. If using sequin *trim*, follow the same steps, but handstitch the trim to the T-shirt.

4 Measure around the neckline of the shirt just below any ribbed band. For the black dress, cut a piece of sequined fabric the neckline measurement x 1⅛". Place a press cloth over the fabric, and press the long edges ¼" to the wrong side. Pin the sequined band to the T-shirt just below the neckband so the narrow edges meet in the center front. Handstitch both long edges of the fabric band to the T-shirt just below the ribbed band. Use loose stitches so the neckline will still stretch over the child's head. For the white dress, use the narrower sequin trim and follow the same instructions.

5 Measure the center front of the T-shirt from the top of the sequin band to 1" from the hem. For the black dress, cut a piece of sequin fabric the center front length measurement + 1" x 2½" wide. Place a press cloth over the trim, and press the long edges and one short edge ¼" to the wrong side. Pin the pressed sequin trim to the center front of the T-shirt, positioning the narrow pressed edge just under the ribbed neckband to cover the edges of the neckline trim, as in the photograph. (Note that the band won't reach the bottom of the shirt; the raw end will be covered with additional trim in a later step.) Machine or handstitch the edges in place. For the white dress, use the wider sequin trim and follow the same instructions.

6 If desired, sew sequin trim or sequined fabric around the bottom edges of the sleeves.

7 Pin two pockets with the right sides together; sew around the edges, leaving a 3" opening on one side. Trim the corners and turn the pocket right side out. Press the seam allowances at the opening to the inside of the pocket (the opening will be stitched shut when pockets are attached to dress). Repeat with the remaining two pocket pieces. For the black dress, cut two 4½" x 1¼" pieces of sequined fabric and press all the edges ¼" to the wrong side. Press the sequin pieces in half, wrong sides together, and slide them over the top edge of the pockets. Edgestitch the sequined fabric in place. For the white dress, use the narrower sequin trim and follow same steps, handstitching the trim along the upper edge of each pocket.

Uptown Girl

8 Pin the pockets to the T-shirt 4" from the bottom and 1" to 2" from the center band. Edgestitch the pockets along the lower edges and sides.

Sewing the Dress

9 With right sides together, pin and stitch the shorter edges of the skirt pieces together to form a circle. Narrow-hem (page 11) the bottom edge. Measure and mark the center front, center back, and sides of the skirt as on page 12. Run two rows of gathering stitches along the top edge (see pages 11–12 for how to gather).

10 Turn the T-shirt wrong side out and mark a stitching placement line 2" from the bottom edge.

11 Pull the gathering stitches so the skirt fits the bottom of the T-shirt and the markings align. Pin the right side of the skirt to the wrong side of the T-shirt so the top edge of the skirt is along the marked line. Adjust the gathers and stitch the skirt to the T-shirt.

12 For the black dress, cut sequined fabric 2" wide by the circumference of the T-shirt plus 1" and press the long edges and one short edge ¼" to the wrong side. Pin the fabric to the T-shirt so it covers the stitching done in Step 11 and the bottom edge of the center front trim, about 1" from the bottom of the shirt (overlapping the narrow ends at one side seam). Machine-stitch or handstitch it in place along both edges. For the white dress, use the wider sequin trim and follow the same instructions.

13 Sew buttons, evenly spacing them along the center band of the T-shirt.✽

Make waves with a fun and frothy frock

❋ ❋ ❋ ❋

Cool Water

This lovely little dress with long ruffles stitches up beautifully in either woven or knit fabrics. We chose a palette of blues and greens inspired by the colors of the Caribbean.

What You'll Need:

- Basic tool kit (page 7)
- T-shirt
- For the stay and ruffles: ½ yard each of five different colors of 45"-wide fabric
- 3 large buttons

Instructions are for sizes Small (Medium, Large, Extra-Large). Sample shown in size Extra-Large.
All seam allowances are ½" unless otherwise noted.

Getting Ready

1 Lay the T-shirt out flat, measure and mark 2½" (3", 3½", 4") down from each underarm seam, and follow the cutting instructions on page 6. Mark the center front and center back of the shirt. Set aside the bottom of the T-shirt to make a small ruffle (see Step 3).

2 Cut the fabric for the stay and ruffles as noted below.

Sizes Small and Medium

For the stay and the top ruffle, cut the length indicated below x 36".
For all the other ruffles, cut the length indicated below x 1 fabric width.

Sizes Large and Extra-Large

For the stay and the top ruffle, cut the length indicated below x 1 fabric width.
For all the other ruffles, cut the length indicated below x 1½ fabric widths.

	S (2/3)	M (4/5)	L (6/6x)	XL (7/8)
Stay	10"	12"	14"	16"
Top ruffle	5"	6"	7"	7½"
Second ruffle	4"	5"	6½"	7"
Third ruffle	5"	6"	7"	7½"
Fourth ruffle	4"	5"	6½"	7"
Fifth ruffle	6"	6"	8"	8"

Cool Water

Sewing the Dress

3 Measure the length of the center front of the T-shirt from the neckline to the cut edge. From the fabric reserved from the bottom of the T-shirt, cut a 3"-wide piece of fabric the center front measurement x 2. To make the front ruffle, narrow-hem (page 11) two long edges and one short edge, then run two rows of gathering stitches down the center of the ruffle piece (see pages 11–12 for how to gather). Pin the finished edge of the ruffle just below the neckband and pull the gathering stitches so the ruffle extends to the bottom of the T-shirt with no gathering for the last 1" (see Figure A). Zigzag stitch the ruffle to the T-shirt between the tow gathering stitches. Remove the gathering stitches.

4 Prepare the five ruffles by stitching pieces as needed, right sides together, to create the widths noted in the chart pn page 83, then stitching each to form a circle. Press the seam allowances to one side. Narrow-hem the bottom edge of each ruffle. Run two rows of gathering stitches along the top edge of each ruffle, except the first (top) ruffle. Divide the ruffles in half and mark the center front and center back of each.

5 Narrow-hem the bottom edge of the stay, then stitch right sides of the short edges together to form a circle (this will become the center back seam). Press the seam allowance to one side.

6 Arrange the ruffles on the stay, with the fifth ruffle ½" from the bottom edge and the first ruffle even with the top edge. Adjust the placement of the other ruffles so each covers the raw edge of the ruffle below it. Measure and mark the placement lines on the stay.

7 Pull the gathers on the bottom ruffle and pin it with right sides together to the bottom edge of the stay. Adjust the gathers so the center fronts and backs align. Stitch. Press the ruffle down.

8 Repeat with the fourth, third, and second ruffles, gathering and stitching each with the wrong side against the right side of the stay, aligning the top edge of each with its placement line.

9 Pin the top ruffle to the top edge of the stay, with the wrong side of the ruffle against the right side of the stay. Run two rows of gathering stitches through both layers. With right sides together, pin the skirt to the bottom of the T-shirt, aligning center markings and adjusting the gathers so they're evenly distributed. Stitch the seam, catching the bottom edge of the ruffle on the T-shirt in the seam. Sew buttons, evenly spaced, along the center of the T-shirt ruffle.❖

Pretty in Pink

Shades of pink and green in quilting cottons make this simple dress look casual and comfy, while yo-yo flowers give it a whimsical touch.

A trio of pretty tiers just right for twirling

What You'll Need:

- Basic tool kit (page 7)
- T-shirt
- For the skirt:
see Figure A (below) and the yardage chart (right) for Fabrics 1, 2, and 3
- For the yo-yo flowers: yo-yo maker and 5 small buttons

Instructions are for sizes Small (Medium, Large, Extra-Large). Sample shown in size Medium. All seam allowances are ½" unless otherwise noted.

45"-wide fabric	S (2/3)	M (4/5)	L (6/6x)	XL (7/8)
Fabric 1 (top tier, sleeve ruffles, yo-yos)	¼ yard	¼ yard	¼ yard	¼ yard
Fabric 2 (middle tier, yo-yo)	⅓ yard	½ yard	½ yard	½ yard
Fabric 3 (lower tier, hem band, yo-yos)	⅔ yard	⅔ yard	⅔ yard	¾ yard

Getting Ready

1 Lay the T-shirt out flat, measure and mark 3½" (4", 4½", 4½") down from each underarm seam, and follow the cutting instructions on page 6. Mark the center front and center back of the shirt. Measure, mark, and cut off 2" from the bottom edge of each sleeve.

2 Cut one or two fabric strips for the tiers and hem band as follows:

	S (2/3)	M (4/5)	L (6/6x)	XL (7/8)
Top tier	(1) 5" x 31"	(1) 6" x 33"	(1) 7" x 35"	(1) 7½" x 37"
Middle tier	(2) 6" x 25"	(2) 7" x 26"	(2) 8" x 26"	(2) 8½" x 27"
Lower tier	(2) 8" x 37"	(2) 9" x 38"	(2) 10" x 39"	(2) 10½" x 40"
Hem band	(2) 3" x 37"	(2) 3" x 38"	(2) 3" x 39"	(2) 3" x 40"

For the sleeve ruffles, measure the circumference of the bottom edge of the sleeve. Cut two fabric strips twice the sleeve circumference x 4" wide. Save the remnants for the yo-yos.

Pretty in Pink

Sewing the Dress

3 With right sides together, sew the two pieces for the middle tier together and the two pieces for the lower tier together on both short edges to form two circles. Also with right sides together, sew the short edges of the top tier together to form a circle. Stitch two rows of basting stitches along one long edge of each tier. (See pages 11–12 for how to gather.)

4 With right sides together, pin the basted edge of the middle tier to the bottom edge of the top tier, adjusting the basting stitches so the middle tier aligns with the top tier. Stitch. Repeat to stitch the basted edge of the lower tier to the bottom edge of the middle tier. Press the seam allowances toward the top of the skirt.

5 With right sides together, sew the two hem band pieces together along both short edges to make a circle. With wrong sides together, press the hem band in half, then press one long edge ½" to the wrong side.

6 Unfold the hem band. With the right side of the hem band facing the wrong side of the lower tier, pin the unpressed edge of the hem band to the bottom edge of the lower tier. Align the seams of the hem band with the seams of the lower tier as closely as possible. Stitch.

7 Fold the hem band along the pressed creases to the right side of the skirt. Edgestitch through all the layers, close to the loose fold, to hold the band in place.

8 Adjust your sewing machine to a stretch stitch (if it doesn't have one, use a zigzag stitch). With right sides together, pin the top edge of the top tier to the bottom of the shirt, adjusting the gathers to fit the shirt. Stitch.

9 With wrong sides together, sew each sleeve ruffle piece into a circle along the short edges. Press the ruffles in half with wrong sides together. Sew two rows of basting stitches along the unfinished edge (through both layers) of each ruffle.

10 Pin the unfinished edges of the ruffles to the right side of the bottom edge of the sleeves, adjusting the gathering stitches. Adjust your sewing machine to a stretch (or zigzag) stitch and sew. Remove all the basting threads. Press the seams toward the shirt.

11 Following the instructions that come with the yo-yo maker, make five yo-yos with leftover fabric. Sew a button in the center of each yo-yo; with the same thread, sew the yo-yos along the neck edge of the shirt.

A sweet treat for a little hostess with the mostest

What's Cooking

Leftover bits of coordinating prints or a charm pack can transform a T-shirt into an apron dress brimming with retro charm.

You'll Need:

- Basic tool kit (page 7)
- T-shirt
- For the bodice and trim: 5 to 6 fat quarters
- For the apron: ⅓ yard 45"-wide fabric
- For the hem band: ¼ yard 45"-wide fabric
- For the skirt: 1 yard 45"-wide fabric
- 1½ yards lace trim
- 1 package rickrack
- Double-sided, paper-backed fusible web

Instructions are for sizes Small (Medium, Large, Extra-Large). Sample shown in size Medium. All seam allowances are ½" unless otherwise noted.

Getting Ready

1 Lay the T-shirt out flat, measure and mark 2" (2", 3", 3½") down from each underarm seam, and follow the cutting instructions on page 6. Mark the center front and center back of the shirt. Save the bottom of the T-shirt to line the top of the dress if using a thin T-shirt (optional).

2 Cut the following pieces as indicated:

Straps: Cut two, each 18" x 5" (longer for a particularly tall child).
Front panel: Cut one, 2½" wide x length of the cut T-shirt at center front.
Side front panels: Cut 2, each 1" wide x length of the cut T-shirt at center front.
Binding strips: Cut one, 1" wide x approximately 36" to bind armholes and neckline.
Waistband: Cut one, 2½" wide x circumference of the T-shirt bottom edge + 1".
Sash: Cut two, each 4" x 22".

Skirt and hem band width: Measure the circumference of the bottom of the cut off T-shirt and multiply that number by 3.
Apron width: Cut one fabric width.
Lengths: See chart below:

	S (2/3)	M (4/5)	L (6/6x)	XL (7/8)
Skirt	13"	13½"	14½"	15½"
Hem band	5"	5"	5"	5"
Apron	10"	10½"	11½"	12"

What's Cooking

(A)

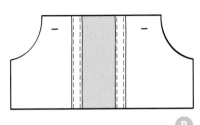

(B)

(C)

❋ **TIP**
If the T-shirt is thin, consider using the cut-off bottom of the shirt to face or self-line it.

Making the Top

3 Mark the neckline cutting lines on the T-shirt by drawing a line straight across the front and back of the T-shirt just below the ribbed neckband and inside the sleeve seam. Cut along the marked lines (see Figure A).

4 Sew the right side of the side front panels to the wrong side of front panel. Press the seams toward the center and the remaining longer edge of each side front panel ¼" to the wrong side. Press the folded edge over the seam to cover it and edgestitch the side panels in place.

5 Pin the panel to the center of the T-shirt and edgestitch it in place. Mark buttonholes about 2" down from the top edge and in the center between the panel and the armhole. Fuse a small piece of fusible web behind the buttonhole marking and make two horizontal buttonholes about ½" long (see Figure B).

6 Press one long edge of the binding strip to the wrong side. Bind the front neck and armhole edges by pinning the right side of the binding strip to the wrong side of the T-shirt, then stitch. Press and fold the strip over the seam, then edgestitch the folded edge in place on the right side of the T-shirt. Don't bind the back neck edge yet.

7 Fold each of the strap pieces in half lengthwise, right sides together, and stitch the long edge. Turn the strap right side out, center the seam, and press. Press the raw edges at one end of each strap ¼" to the inside and edgestitch them in place. Position the unfinished edges of the straps on the back neck edge of the T-shirt, about 1" from each side; with the seams facing up and raw edges aligned, baste them in place. Then bind the back neck edge as in Step 6, including the strap edges in the seam (see Figure C).

8 With right sides together, join the waistband pieces to make a circle. Also with right sides together, pin one long edge of the waistband to the bottom edge of the T-shirt and stitch; press. Set the top aside.

Making the Skirt

9 Narrow-hem (page 11) the bottom and sides of the apron. Edgestitch a piece of lace trim or eyelet 3½" up from the bottom edge across the width of the apron. Cut a decorative strip of remnant fabric 1½" x 45". Press all edges ¼" to the wrong side and edgestitch the strip in place just over the top edge of the trim. Run two rows of gathering stitches across the top of the apron.

What's Cooking

10 With right sides together, sew the skirt pieces together and the hem band pieces together to form circles. Press the bottom of the hem band ½" to the wrong side. Pin the remaining side of the hem band to the bottom of the skirt with the right sides together and stitch. Press the folded edge of the hem band to the wrong side so it covers the seam and stitch it in place. Edgestitch rickrack to the right side of the skirt directly over the seam.

11 Run two rows of gathering stitches across the top of the skirt, pull the gathers so the skirt fits the bottom of the waistband (see pages 11–12). Also pull the gathers on the apron so it fits in the center of the T-shirt, about 2" from each side seam. Baste the top of the skirt and the top of the apron together.

12 Pin the skirt/apron to the bottom of the waistband with right sides together. Stitch all the layers together. Press.

13 Narrow-hem both long edges and one short edge of each sash. Fold a pleat in one short edge and pin it to the right side of the waistband at the side seam, extending the sash toward the front of the dress. Stitch it in place, then fold the sash over the seam (extending it toward the back) and edgestitch again close to the fold to hide the raw edge.

14 To wear the dress, insert the straps through the buttonholes and tie the ends in decorative knots.❊

❊ **TIP**
If desired, cut a second waistband and use it to line the waistband and cover the seams.

For the Frill of It

Rows of mini-ruffles transform a basic T-shirt into a great dress for kicking up her heels. Finish with a fabric sash, or simply tie a pretty white ribbon around the waist.

A yummy confection of sweet mini-ruffles

What You'll Need:

- Basic tool kit (page 7)
- T-shirt
- For the underskirt and ruffles: see yardage chart (right)

Instructions are for sizes Small (Medium, Large, Extra-Large). Sample shown in size Small. All seam allowances are ½" unless otherwise noted.

45"-wide fabric	S (2/3)	M (4/5)	L (6/6x)	XL (7/8)
Underskirt	½ yard	½ yard	½ yard	¾ yard
Ruffles	1 yard	1 yard	1½ yards	1½ yards

Getting Ready

1 Lay the T-shirt out flat, measure and mark 3" (3½", 4", 4") down from each underarm seam, and follow the cutting instructions on page 6. Mark the center front and center back of the shirt.

2 Measure the circumference of the bottom edge of the T-shirt and multiply by 1½ to determine the desired cutting width of the underskirt. Refer to the chart below for the cutting length.

	S (2/3)	M (4/5)	L (6/6x)	XL (7/8)
Skirt length	12"	13"	14"	16"

3 Each ruffle is 2" long x two fabric widths wide. Make as many ruffles as indicated in the chart below, or adjust the number to better fit your child. Cut two pieces of fabric for each ruffle required.

	S (2/3)	M (4/5)	L (6/6x)	XL (7/8)
Number of ruffles	8	9	10	11

For the Frill of It

Sewing the Dress

4 To make each ruffle, sew two ruffle pieces right sides together at both narrow ends to make circles. Narrow-hem (see page 11) one long edge. Set one ruffle aside to use as the top ruffle. On all remaining ruffles, press the unhemmed edge ½" to the wrong side.

5 With right sides together, sew the underskirt pieces together to make a circle. Narrow-hem the bottom edge. Mark the center front and center back of the underskirt.

6 Mark the center front and center back of one ruffle. Run one row of gathering stitches ¼" from the folded edge (see pages 11–12 for how to gather). Pull the gathers and pin the ruffle to the bottom edge of the underskirt, directly over the hemmed edge. Adjust the gathers so the center markings align and edgestitch the ruffle in place.

7 Mark and gather the rest of the ruffles. Pin the next ruffle on the underskirt so the bottom edge of the ruffle is approximately ½" above the top edge of the first ruffle. Edgestitch it in place, same as for first ruffle.

8 Continue stitching all the ruffles in place until the entire underskirt is covered. Space the ruffles evenly; occasionally measure the side seams to check spacing. As you near the top edge, adjust the placement and spacing as needed so the top ruffle is placed even with the top edge of the skirt. Baste the raw edges of the top ruffle and underskirt together.

9 Run two rows of gathering stitches across the top of the skirt. Pull the stitches so the top of the skirt fits the bottom of the T-shirt. Pin the two with the right sides together, adjusting the gathers so the centers align and the gathers are evenly distributed. Stitch. Remove any visible gathering stitches. Press.

10 Tie a ribbon at the waist or make a double fabric sash (see page 15). If desired, tack the sash to the dress at the side seams to keep it from slipping. ✽

Banner Day

Making this sweet but simple dress—a gathered skirt bedecked with little banners "strung" on bias binding—will give both you and your little girl something to celebrate.

Get festive with prints in her favorite colors

What You'll Need:

- Basic tool kit (page 7)
- T-shirt or tank top
- For the skirt: 1¼ (1¼, 1½, 1½) yards 45"-wide fabric
- For the banners: 6 fat quarters OR one charm pack
- Banner template (page 18)
- 2 packages extra-wide double-fold bias binding
- 1 package jumbo rickrack

Instructions are for sizes Small (Medium, Large, Extra-Large). Sample shown in size Large. All seam allowances are ½" unless otherwise noted.

Getting Ready

1 Lay the tank top out flat, measure and mark 4½" (5", 5½", 6") down from each underarm seam, and follow the cutting instructions on page 6. Mark the center front and center back of the shirt.

2 Measure the circumference at the bottom edge of the T-shirt or tank top and multiply by 2 to determine the cutting width for the skirt. If necessary, cut two pieces and stitch them together to get the desired width. Refer to the chart below for the length measurements.

	S (2/3)	M (4/5)	L (6/6x)	XL (7/8)
Skirt length	16"	19"	20"	22"

3 For the waistband, add 2" to one half of the circumference measurement in Step 2. Choose one of the fabrics and cut it into 3"-wide strips. Sew as many as needed with right sides together to obtain the desired length for the front waistband.

4 For the sashes, cut two pieces, each 4" x 18". (Use the same fabric as the waistband if there's enough fabric remaining.)

5 Using the template provided (see page 18), cut 50 to 60 banner pieces to make 25 to 30 banners. Adjust the number of banners as needed to fit the size of the dress.

Sewing the Dress

6 With right sides together, sew the skirt pieces to form a circle. Narrow-hem (page 11) the bottom edge, then topstitch rickrack over the hemmed edge.

Banner Day

7 Make a banner by sewing two pieces with right sides together, leaving the shorter edge unstitched. Trim the seam allowances, turn right side out, and press. Repeat to make the remaining banners.

8 Using the photograph at left as a reference, chalk-mark two placement lines on the skirt that run all the way around it. Draw the placement line at least 1" from the top edge and at least 5" from the bottom edge.

9 Starting at the center back, place the folded edge of a long length of bias binding along the top placement line, then slide the raw edge of one banner between the folds of the bias binding and pin both in place. Continue sliding banners in and pinning binding over their raw edges, overlapping the raw edges slightly all the way around. Edgestitch both long edges of the bias binding to the skirt, catching the raw edges of all the banners in the seams. Repeat along the second placement line.

10 Run two rows of gathering stitches along the top edge of the skirt (see pages 11–12 for how to gather); measure and mark the centers and sides (page 12). With right sides together, pin the top edge of the skirt to the bottom edge of the T-shirt, matching the markings and adjusting the gathers; stitch. Press the seam toward the shirt.

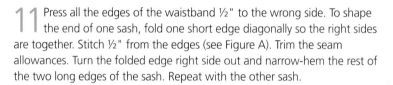

A

11 Press all the edges of the waistband ½" to the wrong side. To shape the end of one sash, fold one short edge diagonally so the right sides are together. Stitch ½" from the edges (see Figure A). Trim the seam allowances. Turn the folded edge right side out and narrow-hem the rest of the two long edges of the sash. Repeat with the other sash.

12 Pin the wrong side of the waistband to the right side of the dress front so the bottom folded edge of the waistband just covers the waistline seam. Pin a small pleat in the unfinished edge of each sash and pin them to the dress just under the narrow edges of the waistband at the side seams. Edgestitch all around the waistband, catching the edges of the sash in the stitching.

13 To make a flower (optional), use the template (page 18) to cut 12 petals from the leftover fabrics. With the right sides of two petals together, stitch two sides, leaving the base of the triangle unstitched. Trim the seam allowances and turn the petals right side out. Repeat with the remaining petals.

14 Pin the unfinished edges of the six petals so they overlap, then baste them together. Run a row of gathering stitches along the basting stitches. Pull the gathers so the petals form a circle with all the unfinished edges in the center. Sew zigzag stitches randomly over the unfinished edges to sew the petals together and cover the raw edges. Cover the zigzag stitches with a large button. Sew the flower to the T-shirt.❉

Tutu Cute

This frothy confection will inspire your little star, from her first plié to her curtain call.

For tiny dancers and aspiring ballerinas

What You'll Need:

- Basic tool kit (page 7)
- T-shirt
- For the underskirt: ½ yard cotton knit fabric
- For the tulle overskirt: 2 rolls precut tulle, 6" wide (sizes Small and Medium) OR 8" wide (Large and Extra-Large)
- For the waistband: 1 package extra-wide, double-fold bias binding OR a fabric remnant 2" x 32" (Small and Medium) or 2" x 42" (Large and Extra-Large)
- ¾ yard ½"-wide elastic
- Safety pin

Instructions are for sizes Small (Medium, Large, Extra-Large). Sample shown in size Small. All seam allowances are ½" unless otherwise noted.

Getting Ready

1 Lay the T-shirt out flat, measure and mark 6½" (6½", 7½", 7½") down from each underarm seam, and follow the cutting instructions on page 6. Mark the center front and center back of the shirt.

2 Cut a piece of knit fabric as an underskirt for the layers of tulle. Refer to the chart below for the cutting measurements.

	S (2/3)/M(4/5)	L (6/6x)/XL(7/8)
Fabric width	32"	42"
Fabric length	10"	14"

3 Cut the tulle into strips as indicated below. (If you're using rolls of tulle, simply cut the strips to the required length; if you're using yardage, you'll need to cut and piece enough strips to obtain the desired width.)

	S (2/3)/M(4/5)	L (6/6x)/XL(7/8)
Number of strips	3	4
Size of strips	6" x 50" (150" in total)	8" x 50" (200" in total)

Sewing the Dress

4 Fold each strip of tulle in half lengthwise to create a double layer. Mark the halfway point of each strip. Run one line of gathering stitches close to the fold (see pages 11–12 for how to gather).

Tutu Cute

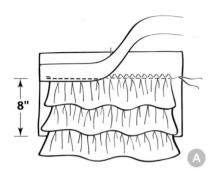

8"

5 Lay out the fabric for the underskirt. Mark the center and draw horizontal lines across the width for the placement of each of the tulle layers. Mark the first line 4" up from the bottom, and then every 2" up from that first line (three lines for Small and Medium, four lines for Large and Extra-Large).

6 Pull the gathering stitches on one layer of tulle to match the size of the underskirt; adjust the gathers so the center markings align. Pin the tulle to the underskirt along the bottom placement line, starting and stopping ½" from each side (for seam allowance). Stitch it in place close to the fold. Repeat with the remaining layers of tulle.

7 Cut a piece of bias binding or remnant fabric equal to the width of the underskirt and press it open. Press one long edge ¼" to the wrong side. Pin the folded edge directly over the seam, attaching the top tulle layer to the underskirt as shown in Figure A. Stitch the binding in place, starting and stopping the stitching ½" from each side to form a waistline casing.

8 With right sides together, pin the center back seam. Stitch from the bottom of the skirt up to the bottom of the binding, taking care to keep the tulle layers out of the seam. Also with right sides together, stitch the ends of the binding together; do not catch the underskirt in the seam (the binding becomes a waistline casing for elastic and the underskirt becomes the facing for the casing). The center back seam of the underskirt is not stitched; it remains open so you can insert elastic into the casing.

9 Mark the center front of the casing and run two rows of gathering stitches close to the top edge. Pull the gathering stitches so the top of the casing aligns with the bottom edge of the T-shirt. With right sides together, pin the casing to the T-shirt, keeping the underskirt out of the seam. Adjust the gathers so the markings align and the gathers are evenly distributed. Stitch. Press the seam toward the hem.

10 Extend the top edge of the underskirt up to cover the seam and act as a facing to the casing. Hand- or machine-stitch the underskirt to the casing by stitching directly over seam stitched in Step 9 (the center back of the underskirt is still not stitched). If the underskirt extends beyond the stitching, trim it away.

11 Measure the child's waist and cut a piece of elastic to that measurement + 1". Attach one end to a safety pin and use it to insert the elastic in the casing through the center back. Overlap the ends of the elastic, stitch them together, and slide them back into the casing.

12 Cut the hem edge of all the tulle layers into an uneven "sawtooth" hemline. No need to measure; just cut out evenly spaced triangles.✢

Cat's Meow

A trendy one-shoulder silhouette, leopard-print fabric, touches of purple, ruffles, and a fancy flower pin—what's not for a little girl to love?

Tailor-made for a walk on the wild side

What You'll Need:

- Basic tool kit (page 7)
- T-shirt
- For the skirt:
1½ yards 45"-wide fabric
- For the skirt ruffle:
1 yard 45"-wide fabric
- 1 package extra-wide double-fold bias tape (in the same color as the T-shirt)
- ½ yard ½"-wide elastic
- Embroidery thread (in a color that contrasts with both the T-shirt and the skirt fabric)
- For the layered fabric flower (optional): scraps of fabric and tulle, ½" round button, and pin back; see template on page 17

Instructions are for sizes Small (Medium, Large, Extra-Large). Sample shown in size Small. All seam allowances are ½" unless otherwise noted.

Getting Ready

1 Lay the T-shirt out flat, measure and mark 4½" (5", 5½", 5½") down from each underarm seam, and follow the cutting instructions on page 6. Mark the center front and center back of the shirt. Set aside the bottom of the T-shirt. Cut the sleeves off the T-shirt, removing the seam and seam allowances; set aside the sleeves. Try the shirt on the child and chalk-mark a diagonal cutting line from the right shoulder to approximately the middle of the armhole (see Figure A). Take the shirt off and even out the line. Cut just above the marked line.

4½"

The cutting line will be somewhat diagonal depending on the neckline of the T-shirt. Cut slightly above the line, trimming away any neckline stitching or ribbing, then try the shirt on the child to see if any

(A) adjustments are needed.

2 To prepare the ruffles for the top, cut open the sleeves and the bottom of the T-shirt and press flat; trim off the seam allowances. Cut crosswise into 2"-wide strips. Measure the cut edge of the neckline; stitch together the strips as needed to make three strips that are each twice as long as the neckline measurement. Stitch the short edges of each ruffle together to make three circles.

Cat's Meow

TIP
If you're working with lightweight T-shirt fabric, stabilize the folded edge by inserting a narrow strip of fabric or interfacing inside it before stitching through all the layers.

3 Measure the circumference of the bottom edge of the T-shirt. Multiply by 2 to determine the fabric cutting width for the skirt, and multiply by 4 for the skirt ruffle. Refer to the chart below for the length measurements.

	S (2/3)	M (4/5)	L (6/6x)	XL (7/8)
Skirt	10"	12"	13"	15"
Skirt ruffle	5"	5"	6"	6"

Sewing the Dress

4 Apply bias tape around the armhole (page 14), overlapping the ends near the underarm.

5 Press one long edge of each ruffle ½" to the wrong side. Thread your sewing machine with decorative embroidery thread. Choose a decorative stitch (or an overedge or zigzag stitch) and stitch along the folded edge. Press the narrow edges ¼" to the wrong side and edgestitch them in place. Run two rows of gathering stitches along the remaining long edge (see pages 11–12 for how to gather).

6 Use a fabric-marking pen or chalk to draw three ruffle-placement lines parallel to the cut neckline. Start with the first line ¾" below the cut edge, then draw the lines about ¼" apart.

7 Pull up the gathering stitches on the shirt ruffles so they're the same length as the neckline, then pin one along the bottom placement line. Adjust the gathers so they're even and stitch along the gathering stitches to attach the bottom ruffle. Repeat with center and top ruffles so the gathered edge of the top ruffle is aligned with the cut edge of the shirt.

8 Finish the entire neckline with double-fold bias tape (see page 14). Start in the back near the underarm seam of the shirt, catching the upper edge of the top ruffle in the seam and encasing the cut neckline with the bias tape. Overlap the ends of the tape to finish.

9 With right sides together, sew the center back seam of the skirt (or, if there are two skirt pieces, sew the side seams). Zigag or overlock the top edge of the skirt, then press it ½" to the wrong side. Stitch the same decorative stitch from Step 5 along the folded edge. Narrow-hem (see page 11) the bottom edge. Run two rows of gathering stitches below the decorative top edge. Measure and mark the centers and side seams of the skirt (see page 12).

Cat's Meow

10 Pull the gathering stitches so the skirt fits the bottom edge of the T-shirt. (See pages 11–12 for how to gather.) Draw a placement line 1½" from the bottom of the shirt and position the skirt (with the wrong side of skirt over the right side of T-shirt) so the gathering stitches are directly over the placement line. Align the markings and adjust the gathers so they're evenly distributed. Stitch. Remove the gathering stitches if they're visible.

11 With right sides together, stitch the skirt ruffle pieces to form a circle. Sew a narrow hem (see page 11) on the bottom edge. Measure and mark the centers and side seams (see page 12). Run two rows of gathering stitches across the top edge and pull the gathers so the markings on the ruffle and the bottom of the skirt align. Slide the gathered edge of the ruffle under the bottom of the skirt (with the right side of the ruffle to the wrong side of the skirt) so the top edge of the ruffle is 1½" above the bottom edge of the skirt. Stitch the ruffle in place, aligning the stitching between the two rows of gathering stitches.

12 For the shoulder strap (optional), cut a piece of fabric 2" x 16" (trim to desired length later). Fold the strip in half, right sides together, and stitch the long edges together with ¼" seam allowances. Turn the strip right side out. Attach a safety pin to the elastic and run it through the strip. Baste one end of the elastic to one end of the strip. Pin the strap to the dress and try it on the child. Adjust as needed, then stitch both ends to the dress; trim away any excess strap.

13 To make the layered fabric flower (optional), photocopy and cut out the template (see page 17). Using a combination of skirt fabric, ruffle fabric, and tulle, trace and cut out 12 to 14 flowers. Layer the flowers so the petals are misaligned slightly, then handstitch through center to secure the layers. Fold the flower in half on itself, then in half again to create a point at the back; machine-stitch ¼" from the point. Open the flower flat and spread out the petals. Handsew a button in the center and the pin back on the back. ✻

Royal Wedding

Layers of ruffles and lace transform a simple white T-shirt into a dress fit for a queen—or the little princess in your life.

Perfect for all sorts of celebrations (and playing dress-up)

What You'll Need:

● Basic tool kit (page 7)

● T-shirt

● For the stay, ruffles, and overskirt: see the yardage chart (right)

● To finish and trim the neckline: 1 yard each: 2"-wide double layer lace trim and ¼"-wide ribbon

● To trim the overskirt: 6 yards 8"-wide flat lace trim

● To trim the waistline and sleeves: 2 yards 1"-wide lace trim

● 5 small premade organza flowers (optional)

Note All trim and fabric yardages are approximate and determined by the desired fullness and length of the skirt. Add more ruffles for a tall child, or use fewer for a shorter one. See Step 2 for further instructions.

Instructions are for sizes Small (Medium, Large, Extra-Large). Sample shown in size Large. All seam allowances are ½" unless otherwise noted.

45"-wide fabric	S (2/3)	M (4/5)	L (6/6x)	XL (7/8)
Cotton broadcloth (stay)	⅓ yard	½ yard	½ yard	¾ yard
Taffeta (ruffles)	2 yards	2 yards	2 yards	2½ yards
Chiffon (overskirt)	2 yards	2 yards	2 yards	3 yards

Getting Ready

1 Lay the T-shirt out flat, measure and mark 3" (for Small and Medium) or 4½" (for Large and Extra-Large) down from each underarm seam, and follow the cutting instructions on page 6. Mark the center front and center back of the shirt.

2 The following fabric-cutting guidelines are for a size Large but can be used for all sizes, since the dress can be longer on a smaller child and shorter on a taller child. You can eliminate or add a ruffle or change the ruffle length to better fit your child. The finished back length of the dress is 28". The dress will fit around the body as long as the T-shirt is the correct size for your child.

Cut fabric as follows:

Stay
Cut 2 in shape of trapezoid, 16" long
Top of piece: half the circumference of the cut-off T-shirt + 1"
Bottom of piece: top measurement + 8"

Ruffles
Top ruffle: 67" x 7½"
Second ruffle: 90" x 7½"
Third ruffle: 90" x 7½"
Bottom ruffle: 112" x 7½"

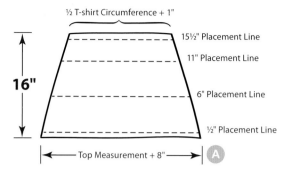

½ T-shirt Circumference + 1"

16"

15½" Placement Line
11" Placement Line
6" Placement Line
½" Placement Line

Top Measurement + 8"

A

Royal Wedding

Making the Skirt

3 With right sides together, pin and stitch the stay pieces at the side seams; press. Use a fabric marking pen or chalk to mark the center front and center back and placement lines on the stay as follows (see Figure A above).

Bottom ruffle: ½" from bottom edge
Third ruffle: 6" from bottom edge
Second ruffle: 11" from bottom edge

4 Make all four ruffles. With right sides together, sew the short edges of each ruffle together to make four circles. Narrow-hem (see page 11) the lower the edge of each ruffle, then run two rows of gathering stitches along the top edge. Divide and mark the top edge of each ruffle in quarters.

5 Gather and pin the bottom ruffle to the bottom edge of the stay, with right sides together and the gathers evenly distributed. Stitch and press.

6 Gather the third ruffle and place it wrong side down on the right side of the stay, so that the top edge of the ruffle is along the placement line 6" from the bottom edge and the ruffle covers the bottom ruffle seam. Approximately 5" of the bottom ruffle will be visible. Stitch.

7 Gather the second ruffle and repeat step 6, placing the ruffle along the placement line 11" from the bottom edge.

8 Gather the top ruffle and align it with the top edge of the stay; stitch. Set the skirt aside.

Making the Top

9 Plan the new neckline for the T-shirt by comparing it to a favorite T-shirt or by placing it on the child. Use chalk or pins to mark the new neckline. Fold the shirt in half lengthwise and adjust the marked lines as needed so the new line is symmetrical. Mark a cutting line ¼" away from this line; cut along the cutting line (see Figure B).

Cutting Line
New Neckline

B

Royal Wedding

10 Starting near one shoulder, zigzag the finished edge of the double-tier lace directly over the marked neckline. Fold the trim slightly at the corners to form a right angle. Continue around the entire neckline (including the back), overlapping the lace ends slightly. Stitch the ribbon over the seam and trim away any visible seam allowance. Press.

11 Mark the desired sleeve length on each sleeve. Cut off the sleeve hem to reduce bulk. Starting at the underarm seam, zigzag the single-layer narrow lace to each sleeve edge at the desired location, overlapping lace ends slightly. Trim away the sleeve below the lace stitching line.

Sewing the Dress

12 With right sides together, gather and stitch the top of the skirt to the bottom edge of the T-shirt, matching center front, center back, and sides (page 12).

13 To make the overskirt, fold the chiffon in half so the selvages are together. Run two rows of gathering stitches along the folded edge, stopping and starting the stitches 1" from each edge. Lay the overskirt over the dress, pinning the folded edge to the waist seam in a few places. Determine the desired length, allowing for a 4"-wide lace ruffle. Also pin or chalk-mark a gentle curve along the center front (as shown in the photo at left). Unpin the chiffon and measure and mark the desired hem length and cut off fabric as needed. Cut along curved lines to create a curved front of the skirt.

Top

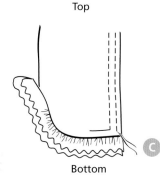

Bottom

14 Fold the wide lace in half and run two rows of gathering stitches along the fold. Pull the gathers gently and start pinning the lace to the overskirt so that the folded edge of the lace is over the cut edge of the skirt (with the wrong side of the lace to the right side of the skirt). Pull the gathers, then pin and continue around the entire outside edge of the overskirt, adjusting the gathers as you pin (see Figure C). Zigzag-stitch the lace in place.

15 Pull the gathers at the top edge of the overskirt and pin it to the waistline seam of the dress (with the wrong side of overskirt to the right side of dress) so that the lace trim overlaps in the center front and the folded edge of the chiffon extends ½" beyond the seam (as shown in the photo directional). Stitch.

16 Starting at a side seam, stitch the narrow lace trim directly over the seam, joining the overskirt to the dress. Overlap the lace ends slightly.

17 To embellish the skirt with small flowers, hand-sew them along the center front of the skirt seam (as shown in the photo on page 109).✳

Resources

Where to Find Fabric

When purchasing fabric, we recommend that you start with your local fabric or quilt shop, where you can consult with their knowledgeable staff on your choices. The following are retail and manufacturers' websites where you can look for fabrics from a variety of companies and designers, find fabrics from independent designers and studios, and research ideas about using and combining fabrics.

Art Galley Fabrics
www.artgalleryfabrics.com

Jimmy Beans Wool
www.jimmybeanswool.com

Connecting Threads
www.connectingthreads.com

Jo-Ann Fabrics and Crafts
www.joann.com

Fabric.com
www.fabric.com

Keepsake Quilting
www.keepsakequilting.com

Fabric Depot
www.fabricdepot.com

Moda Fabrics
www.unitednotions.com

Fat Quarter Shop
www.fatquartershop.com

Robert Kaufman
www.robertkaufman.com

Free Spirit Fabric
www.freespiritfabric.com

Sew Mama Sew
www.sewmamasew.com

Hancock Fabrics
www.hancockfabrics.com

Westminster Fabrics
www.westminsterfabrics.com

Measurement Conversion Chart

Yards to inches to meters

Yards	Inches	Meters
⅛	4.5	.11
¼	9	.23
⅜	13.5	.34
½	18	.46
⅝	22.5	.57
¾	27	.69
⅞	31.5	.80
1	36	.91
1⅛	40.5	1.03
1¼	45	1.14
1⅜	49.5	1.26
1½	54	1.37
1⅝	58.5	1.49
1¾	63	1.60
1⅞	67.5	1.71
2	72	1.83

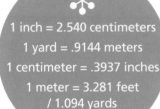

1 inch = 2.540 centimeters
1 yard = .9144 meters
1 centimeter = .3937 inches
1 meter = 3.281 feet / 1.094 yards

Also from Sixth&Spring Books

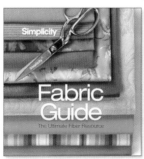

The ultimate fabric reference, from the basics through choosing colors and caring for fabric

From sewing expert Linda Lee, learn to sew in 30 easy projects

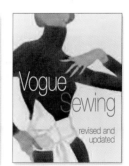

Everything sewers need to create fashionable and professional-looking garments

www.sixthandspringbooks.com

✳ ✳ ✳ ✳ Index